AXIS OF GREATNESS

AXIS OF GREATNESS

MUHAMMAD ALI · ANGELO DUNDEE · SUGAR RAY LEONARD

MIKE WINTERS

BOOKS

First published in Great Britain in 2008 by
JR Books, 10 Greenland Street, London NW1 0ND
www.jrbooks.com

A catalogue record for this book is available from the British Library.

ISBN 978-1-906217-60-0

1 3 5 7 9 10 8 6 4 2

Printed by MPG Books, Bodmin, Cornwall

Contents

Foreword

By Senator John McCain of Arizona

As an avid boxing fan and supporter of the sport – despite the times in its history when it has been 'tarnished' – I have tried to introduce legislation that would help the image of boxing, and more importantly, improve conditions for the fighters.

Exceptional people often transcend their profession, and exceptional boxers can transcend their sport. Even if you do not like boxing, or have never seen a boxing match, it is more than likely you will have heard of Muhammad Ali and Sugar Ray Leonard. Exceptional, charismatic men! Their names will live forever in the hearts of Americans, and for that matter, people throughout the world.

You may or may not have heard of Angelo Dundee, but he is probably the most famous and successful manager/trainer in the annals of boxing history. What magic did he possess that made him the mentor, trainer, corner man and sometimes manager of two such impressive sporting icons?

Axis of Greatness is a book about these three remarkable men and their relationship. Not only is the book about real people, it also shows us some history – the period when the evil tentacles of crime infected the sport, and the repugnant curse of racism rampaged throughout America.

Get ready for a good read and a walk through history with Mike Winters.

Introduction

I have been fortunate in my life to have spent a little time with Angelo Dundee, time that was educational, informative and always fun. I consider Angelo a friend, but I have tried hard not to be biased in my interpretation of the facts. However, I believe Angelo was one of the best things ever to have happened in boxing.

To a lesser extent, I spent some interesting and rewarding times with Muhammad Ali. Those times were always fun, too. I have met royalty, film and stage stars, but among them, Muhammad is the only person I considered to be 'great'. While I didn't have the opportunity to get to know Sugar Ray Leonard, I did spent a lot of time in Angelo's office listening to phone conversations and getting a feeling for their special relationship.

Much of the information I have included in this book comes from my meetings with Angelo's family in South Philadelphia, Pennsylvania, and the many conversations I had with Angelo while researching his biography *I Only Talk Winning*. I have drawn from this source for anecdotes of Angelo's early life because I think they are worth retelling, and those experiences help explain the influences on Angelo's personality. Much of the information in this book comes courtesy of late, acclaimed boxing historian, the late Hank Kaplan, who gave me access to his wonderful archive of boxing news stories and other valuable boxing memorabilia. And, I'd like to thank Walter Bowen for contacting Senator McCain, and for Walter's assistance and encouragement.

If you wonder about my credentials to write this book, let me tell you I grew up in the fight game. My father had about eight pro fights; my uncle on my mother's side, Joe Bloomfield, beat Mike McTigue, the middleweight champion of the world, in a non-title fight. Another of my mother's brothers, known as 'Gentleman' Jack Bloomfield, won the British light heavyweight, and heavyweight titles, and he was awarded the legendary Lonsdale Belt.

I hope you enjoy the read.

Prologue

Though it's a subjective judgement to differentiate between being 'very good' or 'very, very good' or 'great', I don't believe any lovers of the 'sweet science' will argue with my three candidates for the accolade of greatness.

There is no doubt that since 1960 there have been some great fighters and I wouldn't disagree with anyone who included in their list of the top 20 fighters of the past four decades the following – Larry Holmes, Mike Tyson, Roberto Duran, George Foreman, Lennox Lewis, Julio Caesar Chavez, Marco Antonio Barrera, Alexis Arguello, James Tony, Evander Holyfield and Roy Jones Jr. Then there are Sugar Ray Robinson and Rocky Marciano – the undisputed greats of all time.

You could include in your top 20 Marvin Hagler and Thomas 'Hit Man' Hearns, both very good fighters, but Sugar Ray Leonard beat them both in crucial fights. For me, that solidifies his mantle of greatness. Another fighter, former heavyweight champion Pinklon Thomas, never reached the heights or success his skills warranted. He won the title from Tim Witherspoon with just a left jab because his right hand was severely damaged early in the fight.

I haven't made a top 20 list for this book, although it would have been a fun exercise. It's a game maybe you would like to play. If you do, please send me a list and I will compare it to the others, and maybe we can come up with a consensus of the 20 greatest fighters of the last 40 years.

Without a doubt, Oscar De La Hoya, Floyd Mayweather, Sugar Shane Mosley, Bernard Hopkins, Joe Calzaghe and Ricky Hatton have the stamp of greatness. Perhaps they deserve to wear that crown of greatness, and perhaps, that will mean another book down the line.

I presume most of you agree that Muhammad Ali and Sugar Ray Leonard were great, and I think there is no doubt they are the best known boxing names of the past four decades. As Muhammad said, 'I'm the most recognised and loved man that ever lived 'cause there were no satellites when Jesus or Moses lived'. He had a point there.

Sugar Ray Leonard, although never reaching the elevated level of Muhammad Ali, has regained a new kind of fame with his television participation in the successful TV series, *The Contender*. Besides their charismatic personalities, enormous skills and bravery, there is one other major factor that they have in common. In their corner they had probably the best known manager/trainer/cut man in the history of boxing – Angelo Dundee.

Throughout the history of professional sport there has always been the need for a trainer, coach or manager. In boxing, the professional fighter also needs corner men. One of those corner men is a cut man, someone who can repair the cuts, bruising and lacerations that the fighter may get during hard fought rounds. Angelo Dundee is, and has been, an exponent of all those disciplines and skills. Was he good in all of them? Well, besides being in the corner of all of Muhammad Ali's fights and most of Sugar Ray Leonard's, Angelo was also deeply involved in their training, and management. Not only did he work his magic with Ali and Leonard, he was also a major influence in the careers of the following champions – Carmen Basilio (welterweight 1955, middleweight 1957), Luis Rodriguez (welterweight 1963), Sugar Ramos (featherweight 1963), Jose Napoles (welterweight 1969), Willie Pastrano (light heavyweight 1963), Pinklon Thomas (heavyweight 1984) and George Foreman (heavyweight 1973 and 1994). Quite a record! Angelo is our third 'great' in the Axis of Greatness.

Even though the Dundee story started way before he met Muhammad Ali, I believe the logical place to start this tale would be at that first, unforgettable, meeting. It took place in Louisville, Kentucky. Angelo was there with his fighter, Willie Pastrano. There were no plans to meet Ali; in fact, at that time, there was no Muhammad Ali. That name came later, but I'm getting ahead of myself. Let's get back to that first meeting.

CHAPTER 1

'I'm the golden gloves champion of Louisville'

Flying with Willie Pastrano could be a problem. It wasn't so much that he was scared of flying, which he was, it was the female flight attendants, especially if they were pretty, that Angelo had to worry about. He always kept an eye on the good looking fighter in case he tried to persuade one of the young ladies to join him in the rest room. Willie was a fully fledged member of the 'Mile High Club'. Angelo was relieved to see their stewardess was rather homely. He could relax.

It was February 1957 and they were on their way to Louisville where Willie was fighting Johnny Holman. It would be a tough fight. Angelo thought it wise to get Willie away from any temptations, and get in a few extra days training in Louisville instead of flying in on the day of the fight. He could also rustle up some publicity. Willie was headlining. They wanted a full house.

When they arrived at the Louisville gym, the media were waiting for them. The promoter, Bill King, a friendly guy, gave the reporters a quick spiel and introduced Willie to answer their questions. The news guys in Louisville were all big fight fans, and it was unusual to get to talk with the fighter instead of the manager. Angelo didn't like the practice of having the fighter handling the questions by saying something like, 'Ask my manager. I do the fighting, he does the talking.' He thought it belittled the fighter. He didn't want Willie, or any fighter he handled, to come across as a dummy, or cast him in the role of a 'fast talking, anything for a buck' type of manager. Dundee wanted his fighters to talk, to soak up the glamour. He wanted the press and the public to know the fighter, not him. And no one pays to watch a boxing match to see the manager. Willie, with his easy charm and good looks, was a natural. The press loved him, and Willie enjoyed the spotlight. He flirted outrageously with all the female reporters of any age, but always in good taste and always with humour.

The day before the fight after the workout in the gym, Bill King, who was in seventh heaven over the big advance ticket sales, offered to take Willie and Angelo to lunch. Willie politely declined because he wanted to get back to the hotel and watch himself on a lunchtime interview show. After devouring a plate of tagliatelle alla crema, followed by veal pizzaiola, and cheese and celery, washed down by Frascati wine, espresso coffee, and a large grappa, Angelo returned to the hotel happy with the thoughts that he didn't have to watch his weight, and more importantly, he didn't have to fight tomorrow night. Feeling a little guilty, Dundee purposely avoided mentioning the meal to Willie, who was stretched out on the bed watching the last seconds of the talk show.

'How were you?' Angelo asked as the TV credits started to roll.

'Just great. I'm one hell of a handsome Wop,' Willie answered, grinning.

They usually ate around 6.30pm, so they had four or so hours to kill. Willie got his 175–pound frame off the bed and sat in front of the television set and began searching for a programme he liked. Angelo, full and relaxed, head propped up by a couple of pillows, lay on the bed and tried to visualise how the next day's fight would play out. Johnny Holman was good, but Angelo thought Willie's jab and speed would be too much for him. Even so, he was concerned about the height differential – Johnny was nearly 6 feet 6 inches and a fully fledged heavyweight, and Willie, although he had bulked up for the fight, was a natural light heavyweight and not quite 6ft. Angelo had trained both fighters and hoped Willie would be too clever and fast for the taller man.

He looked over at Willie, who was still surfing the channels with no success. Angelo smiled to himself. Willie really was a character. He had specific taste in movies and TV, preferring tough cop stories, or horror shows. In fact, sometimes he would sketch violent scenes, like a guy holding a dagger dripping with blood standing over some scared guy, or terrified gal. He had artistic talent, but he wasn't exactly into pretty landscapes. It's strange that so many fighters draw or paint. You never think of those macho guys being artistic, but many are. The phone interrupted Angelo's musings. Reaching across the bedside table, he picked up the receiver.

'Hello, Angelo here.'

'Hello, my name is Cassius Marcellus Clay. I am the Golden Gloves Champion of Louisville. I won the Atlanta Golden Gloves. I won the Pan American games. I'm gonna be the Olympic Champion, and then I'm gonna be Champion of the Whole World. I'd like to meet you.'

Angelo stared at the telephone in disbelief.

'Who is it?' Willie asked.

'Some nut. He wants to meet me,' Angelo answered. He decided to hear more of the bizarre declaration – you could hardly call it a conversation.

'Well, Mr….huh…huh,' he stammered, struggling to recall the name.

'Mr Cassius Marcellus Clay, Mr Dundee.' Dundee listened for a few minutes and then placed his hand over the receiver and turned to Willie. 'He has his brother with him and they want to come up for five minutes.'

'What the hell,' Willie said. 'Television stinks. Send them up.'

When they entered the room they filled it. They were big boys. Both more than 6 feet 3inches tall. They were slim, but you could tell by looking at them that they were well muscled. Angelo introduced himself and Willie, and Cassius introduced himself and his brother, Rudy. Both young men were very polite. Rudy was carrying a painting and a bust of some guy modelled in clay. It was quite impressive, although neither Willie nor Angelo could figure out its significance. At first, Cassius did most of the talking. He was a likeable guy and he spoke with obvious sincerity.

'I've seen you on the television, Mr Dundee. I saw you with Carmen Basilio, and I saw when Mr Pastrano beat Al Andrews in Chicago. You sure do have one sweet left hand, Mr Pastrano.' Cassius's handsome face broke into a beaming smile.

Willie sat there grinning, trying to appear modest. He ate it up. The five minutes came and went and they were still talking. Willie and Rudy discussed the painting and the bust, and when Cassius joined in he seemed to know what he was talking about. But mainly they talked boxing. Willie and Angelo took over the conversation and the two youngsters listened. The time flew. They were enjoying themselves. Well, there is nothing as interesting as hearing your own voice, on your favourite subject, to a captive audience! After four hours, the Clay boys had to leave. 'Nice guys,' remarked Willie after they had gone.

'Let's eat,' said Angelo, grabbing his jacket.

'Yeah, I'm hungry.' Willie took a quick look in the mirror, ran his fingers through his thick black hair, picked up his jacket and made for the door. 'Nice guys,' he said again.

After he'd made his nightly call to his wife, Helen, Angelo and Willie sat down to a steak dinner. Afterwards, they went for their customary walk. The walk after eating was part of Dundee's training schedule for his fighters. He didn't like them to go to bed on a full stomach. Cassius Marcellus Clay was forgotten. They had other more important things on their minds with the fight less than 24 hours away.

* * *

When the big night arrived, the arena was packed. The full house created its own excitement, and the television cameras angled around the ring to broadcast live boxing from a small town like Louisville gave the noisy crowd a sense of occasion. The extra lighting brought in by the television crew illuminated the ring, making it the focus of attention. Angelo thought, 'This is the way to present boxing.' Little did he dream that within seven years he would be one of the leading players on the stage presenting boxing halfway around the world to an audience of hundreds of millions.

Their changing room was small but clean and in comparison to

5

some of the rooms they had been in, it was a palace.

'How are the bandages?' Dundee asked.

'A little tight,' Willie replied, 'but they're OK.' There was a knock on the door and a voice shouted out that it was time to go.

'Keep moving, he won't touch you,' Angelo said, slapping Willie on the shoulder. 'Let's go.'

The bell sounded and the fight was on. Everything was going according to plan. Willie had made Johnny miss and miss and miss again, but then Johnny didn't miss. Right at the end of the round he caught Willie with a left hook right on the nose, but before Johnny could follow it up, the bell ended the round. Willie sat slumped on his stool and Dundee frantically began working on his nose. It was broken and bleeding badly. He applied some adrenalin chloride 1-1000 onto a cotton swab and squeezed it into the nostrils to stop the bleeding. Quickly he washed the blood from Willie's face and gently applied a thin layer of vaseline over the nose.

'Can you breathe OK?'

'Yeah, I guess so.' Willie looked at Angelo from the corners of his eyes. 'I thought he wouldn't touch me?'

Angelo slapped his cheek and said, 'He didn't touch you, he hit you.' He grinned, putting Willie's gum shield in before the boxer could answer. The bell sounded for the second round. 'Dance, Willie, dance,' Dundee urged. He did. For nine rounds he was immaculate – in and out, dancing away, scoring points with his impeccable left hand. He was the classic boxer. Dundee felt sorry for Johnny. It was like trying to hit a shadow. First Willie was there and then he wasn't.

It was a great fight and the fans loved it. It was no surprise to anyone that at the end of the fight Willie was declared winner on points in a unanimous decision. The crowd was exhausted but jubilant and standing ringside were the Clay brothers leading the cheering.

That night Angelo and Willie had supper with Bill King, the promoter, and a couple of the television production staff. Everyone was in party mood except Willie who, with a broken nose, understandably didn't feel like whooping it up.

The fight had taken the most money in box office receipts in the history of Louisville's boxing promotions. Bill King had been delighted to pay Dundee after the fight. Angelo settled with Willie the following morning. After deducting miscellaneous expenses – travel and hotel costs were paid by the promoter – Angelo took one third. He gave half of it to Willie's old manager who had retained a piece of the action. Angelo had to pay for all personal expenses, such as telephones, drinks, taxis, tips and stuff needed for the corner. There were gauzes, sticky tape, vaseline and the invaluable 1-1000. There were no free samples!

On the plane back to Miami, Angelo told Willie that the first thing they were going to do was to see a doctor and get his nose fixed.

'You know, Angie, I ain't gonna get rich doing this,' Willie said as he carefully touched his nose.

'You and me both, Willie, but what else do we know?'

Willie was thoughtful for a moment. 'I was thinking about that young kid Cassius Clay, just starting out. I wonder if he realises how tough this game is? Plus he's black which is gonna make it even more difficult for him.'

'Yeah, but, if he's got the bug, what can you do? The kid wants to be a fighter.'

'True. Yeah, what you gonna do? D'you think he'll make it?' Willie asked slowly in his soft, New Orleans drawl.

'Who knows? Maybe. The kid sure had somethin' about him, but who the heck knows. This is some crazy game we're in, my friend.'

For a while, they were silent, each lost in their own thoughts. Angelo gave Willie a playful dig in his ribs. 'Hey, Willie, I've got a new welterweight coming to the gym tomorrow. A kid by the name of Luis Rodriguez. He was the Cuban champion. I've seen him fight, and I tell you, he's something else.'

'Yeah? I'll come down and watch him. Maybe I'll do a little shadow boxing. Give the guys a laugh. I had better brush up on my Spanish. Si Señor?'

'Great. Then we'll see the Doc about your nose.'

'Yeah.' Willie was silent for a moment, his thoughts back in Louisville. 'You know something, except for getting nailed in the first round, I was in complete control. Was I good or what?'

'You looked real good. I'll try and get you another fight in Louisville. They love you there.' Angelo smiled.

'That would be good. Maybe we'll see that Cassius Clay kid again. Hey Angie, what makes anyone go into the fight game?'

'Money? Who knows? Maybe it just happens. You know, circumstances.'

CHAPTER 2

'We were never poor, we just didn't have any money'

Angelo was never an aggressive street-smart kid looking for trouble. In fact, it was being picked on by the local bully named Freddy, who called him Fatso, that began Angelo's involvement in boxing. He hated being called Fatso, but he was too scared to do anything about it.

One day Freddy kept on taunting Angelo in front of the other kids. Although they felt sorry for him, they didn't dare interfere. They were also frightened of Freddy. Angelo hoped that if he ignored Freddy he would drop it and move on. But like most bullies, Freddy knew when he had a victim. He began shoving, pushing and slapping him around. Angelo tried to fight back but he was fat, slow and didn't know how to defend himself. He took a beating.

When Angelo got home his mother took one look at him cried out, 'Figlio mia, che cause su chese?' ('My son! What's happened to you?') His brother, Jimmy, heard his mother's anguished cries and hurried into the kitchen. When Angelo told him what had happened, Jimmy rushed out of the house looking for Freddy. Jimmy was a little older but about the same height as Freddy who was quite a bit heavier. Angelo, who had followed his brother out into the street, watched the confrontation and was worried that his slimly built brother was also going to get knocked about by the local bully. He was wrong. Jimmy could box, and he began giving Freddy the beating he deserved.

Angelo was the baby of the family. All his older brothers could fight, and his eldest brother, Joe, was a professional boxer. Joe was already grown up and didn't live at home so Angelo hardly saw him. Another of his other brothers, Chris, who had left home at the age of 15, had only seen Angelo two or three times in his whole life. Chris and Joe were like gods to Angelo, but it was Jimmy, his protector, and later his mentor, who had the young Angelo's deepest love and affection. It was Jimmy who started to take Angelo to the local gym and taught him how to box. It was Jimmy with whom he shared a room, in the house on Morris Street, in the Italian section of South Philadelphia.

Angelo's parents, Angelo and Philomena Mirenda (the Dundee name came later) arrived in America from Calabria, southern Italy in the early 1900s. Angelo Sr slowly learned to make himself understood in his new language, although he had great difficulty reading and writing. Philomena never mastered English and spoke Italian until the day she died, as did many of the immigrants living in the ghettos. The name Mirenda slowly evolved into Marina or Marino, depending on how the government officials deciphered the signature of Angelo Mirenda Sr.

The name Dundee was brought into the family by the eldest brother Joe, the boxer. He chose a non-Italian sounding name for the same reasons as many other Italians and Jews. Primarily, it was because of anti-Italian or Jewish sentiments, and also because the foreign-sounding names were too long and too difficult to pronounce. Joe Mirenda didn't choose the name Dundee by chance. There were, around that time, three famous Dundees in the fight game, but none of them was born with the Scottish name.

One was Samuel Lazarro, who became the world welterweight champion under the name of Joe Dundee in 1927. The second was Vince Dundee, born Vince Lazarro, brother of Samuel Lazarro. Vince became middleweight champion of the world on 30 October 1933. The Lazarro brothers were born in Italy but grew up in the United States. The third Dundee was Joe Carrara, who was very popular in Philadelphia with the Italian fight fans, especially Joe Mirenda. Carrera eventually won the junior lightweight championship of the world in 1921 from George Chaney. Why did Carrara choose the name Dundee? Carrara had two managers: Jimmy Johnston and Scotty Monteith. These two Scottish-Americans probably gave Joe Carrara the idea of changing his fighting name to the Scottish sounding Johnny Dundee. As Joe Marina/Marino was a huge fan of Johnny Dundee, and as there was a history of Dundees as world champions, Joe decided to use the name too. His Mirenda brothers, Chris and Angelo, also adopted the Dundee name, ultimately taking it to new heights of fame in the boxing world.

With the confidence gained from learning how to fight and with the added security of knowing his brother Jimmy was there for him, life became fun for the young Angelo. No longer was he worried about being called Fatso. He developed into a slim young man who took pride in his body. And, as for the usual teenage problems, he was fortunate to have Jimmy to confide in. A special bond grew between them that would last for the rest of their lives and, without even being conscious of it, Jimmy became the quintessential big brother, taking on the role of advisor and mentor. The result of this relationship would eventually show itself in Angelo's personality. His need of a mentor, first fulfilled by Jimmy, later by his much older brother Chris, was eventually taken over by his perfect mate, his wife, Helen.

*   *   *

When Angelo, essentially a gentle man, became involved in the world of professional boxing, a world of violence, brutality and corruption that paradoxically was inhabited by many wonderful people, he developed an empathy with the boxers. Perhaps it was the way he would have related to the kid brother he never had and it is telling that his association with the business side of the fight game was a necessity that he was never fully at ease with it.

He had grown up in difficult financial circumstances. As Angelo once said, 'We were never poor, we just didn't have any money.' The family ate well as his mother was a good cook and was warm and loving to her children. His father's insistence on discipline was not excessive but realistic. He taught his boys to show respect for others and to be loyal to their family. This was instilled in Angelo and stuck with him throughout his life.

Growing up in South Philly with two brothers who were local boxing celebrities, Joe and Chris, gave Angelo a sense of his place in society. He wasn't the celebrity, he was the celebrities' brother, and he felt comfortable in that position. Jimmy taught him that you didn't have to be a big shot to be a respected man. 'Being who you are is okay,' he preached, 'and if you do happen to do well, don't shoot your mouth off. I don't like the "I am" type of guys, the kinda guys who say "I am this", "I am that". Don't tell me how good you are at what you do. Let the product speak for you.' Throughout his life Angelo never became an 'I am' kind of guy.

When Angelo graduated from high school he got a job at a naval aircraft factory. It was at least an hour's drive away, which meant Angelo had to get up very early. Fortunately for him, his youngest sister, Josephine, would wake him each morning. He would struggle out of bed without waking Jimmy, who could sleep through an earthquake, then fall asleep on the car ride to work. On weekends, Angelo would go to Atlantic City with his buddies, chase girls, build up his now muscular body and eat lots of really hot peppers that he loved.

The future was just the future as far as he was concerned. Today was pretty good. That was all that mattered. Jimmy and he had plans, lots of them, but they changed often. It didn't make a lot of difference to either of them because life was fun and they didn't realise life has its own plans. Before they knew it, America was at war and they were in the military.

CHAPTER 3

The loose goose

Angelo often says 'You gotta go with the flow and stay as loose as a goose.' And that's how he intended to behave while he was in the Army. There was no doubt in his mind after Pearl Harbor that this was a fight he wanted to get into but, like millions of other guys, he didn't really want to leave home. He was having fun, but there were more important things to attend to.

In late October 1943 Angelo Marina, later to become Angelo Dundee, reported for duty. Angelo, whether he cares to admit it or not, is a romantic, the type who buys flowers for a girl and has a special song for her. His fantasies extended to the war and he envisioned being sent to some exotic South Sea island or perhaps Rome, where, looking great in full battle dress, he'd be hailed as a hero by the city's beautiful women. The Army had other ideas and sent him from Philadelphia across the Ben Franklin Bridge, to Camp Kilmer, in New Jersey, an induction centre, where they cut his hair, gave him a uniform and tried to decide what to do with him. There wasn't a palm tree or beautiful signorina in sight.

As a result of that disappointment, Angelo's ever-active

imagination began to picture him doing his basic training somewhere cold, damp, muddy, stark and depressing. This time he was pleasantly surprised to find himself in Miami, under the sunny Florida skies. It was love at first sight between Angelo and Miami. There really were palm trees and the weather in November was as near to perfect as one could imagine. Off duty time was a pleasure. There was the service club, where he went bowling with some of his pals, and he turned out for the boxing squad, actually winning a few fights as a welterweight. It didn't take long for the news to get around in the unit that Angelo could take care of himself. As at school, this was useful as there were one or two bullies who picked on the Jewish and Italian guys who, however, knowing of Angelo's prowess in the ring, stayed out of his way. That wasn't the only advantage of being in the boxing squad – instead of Spam he got steak. When basic training was over, he made a promise to himself that he would return to Miami someday. He wasn't quite sure how or when, but he vowed he would come back.

Although Angelo came from an Italian neighbourhood in South Philly, he had no problem making friends with kids from other ethnic neighbourhoods. South Philly was divided in those days: Irish, Jewish, Black and Italian. Each group had their own turf and gangs, though the gangs were different from those of today – drive-by shootings were virtually unheard of and guns weren't used by kids. Angelo made friends with anyone, regardless of their ethnic or religious background. It wasn't a deliberate attempt to counteract racism or bigotry but the result of the lesson his father had taught him – to show other people respect, regardless of where they came from. He either liked them or he didn't.

Being in the Army opened Angelo's eyes to the virulent disease known as racism. After basic training he was shipped out to England and was first stationed in Leicester where he got along well with his fellow GIs and the locals, although sometimes he had a problem understanding their accent – and they had a problem understanding him. Within months he was transferred to Newbury, a quiet town west of London. Again, he got along well with the locals and the guys in his unit. However, this was 1944, when racism in America was rife and the armed forces were largely segregated. There wasn't much for the troops to do in Newbury, which they dubbed the 'cemetery with lights', except attend the Saturday night dance at the local hall. The black servicemen were not allowed to go. Britain, then, didn't have such race problems, and their soldiers were indignant that these young, black men, risking their lives to serve their country, were prevented from attending the only recreation available. They sent letters to the Commanding Officer, and even went as far as arranging a meeting with him. The Commanding Officer knew what would happen if the black GIs went to the dance, mixing with the white GIs from the Deep South. There was no doubt in the Commander's mind that when the Southern boys saw the black GIs dancing and flirting with white girls there would be trouble. So the ban continued.

Angelo spoke about the situation with two of his buddies, two young men from Georgia, expecting them to feel the same way he did. 'Hey, they're GIs just like us. Why shouldn't they be allowed to go to the dance? I bet they're better dancers than we are.' The response he received wasn't what he expected. The venom in their verbal attack on the black soldiers, and the hatred they expressed towards blacks in general, nauseated Angelo. How could they be such nice guys in every other way and still be such bigots? He realised their attitudes had developed over many years of living in a racist society and that he probably couldn't change their minds. Still, in his own small way he would try. Unfortunately, it simply soured his friendship with his two Georgia pals and it came as a relief when he was eventually transferred to another base.

Later in life, when he had reached a level of success and fame, a reporter asked Angelo why he had trained so many black fighters. Angelo replied, 'If a boxer from Mars wanted me to handle him, as long as the guy could fight I wouldn't care if he was green.'

In 1944, Angelo got some good news. His brother Jimmy, now Sergeant James Marina (Angelo at that time was a PFC or Private First Class), came to visit him and gave him some unexpected news from home. Angelo and Jimmy had received a review in the *Navy Yard Beacon*. The newspaper article reported that the two brothers were active in service boxing. Angelo had boxed while stationed in Miami and both brothers had bouts on their bases in England, but nothing of consequence. Their brother, Chris, probably gave the local newspaper the story and a photograph, wanting to help his brothers. Jimmy had other exciting news to tell his brother.

They were both going to be attached to the United States Air Force Boxing Tournament as corner men. Jimmy didn't know why they had been picked, but they were elated. The orders came through quickly and, before they knew it, Angelo and Jimmy reported to the designated venue for the boxing tournament. After reporting to the sergeant in charge of arrangements for all European Theater of Operations (ETO) Tournaments, they learned they had been chosen because they were Chris Dundee's brothers. Chris was the manager of the former middleweight champion of the world, Ken Overlin, who was serving in the Navy. Jimmy and Angelo felt a sense of pride for their brother, Chris, and gratitude too. It was great having a celebrity as a brother. The Dundee brothers were pleased with what the sergeant told them and the Air Corps were proud to have two corner men like the Dundee boys to help the Air Corps boxers. They had the Dundee brothers working the corner – what could go wrong. No one bothered to inform the brass that their real name was Mirenda – they only cared about the name Dundee.

The next day when they were in the locker room changing for the corner work, Angelo and Jimmy could hardly suppress their smiles. The brass thought they were *experienced* corner men. All they knew about corner work had been picked up by watching at their local South Philly gym, and having corner men when they boxed. How difficult could it be? The Dundee brothers would ace it. Experienced corner men? No problem!

The tournament began and somehow the Dundee brothers got through it. However, it was a case of the blind leading the blind. Jimmy was cool and somehow gave the impression he knew exactly what he was doing, although he was a little over-enthusiastic with the sponge work and practically gave one of the fighters a shower. Angelo tried to follow his example, except he was more prudent with the water sponge. The boxers didn't notice. They were amateurs, and some had never been in a ring before and probably knew less than the Dundee brothers. They thought that their corner men, part of the Dundee family, were the experts. Chris Dundee's reputation, manager of a world champion, had brainwashed them. Little did Angelo realise that the experience he was gaining in the forces would later serve him well.

Angelo returned to the base in Newbury with a new attitude. The

ETO boxing duty had given him an extra boost in confidence. He had no time to worry about the duties he was given, mainly because he was now being sent all over Britain, to different bases, for boxing tournaments. It was an added pleasure for him to be working with his brother Jimmy. They would often meet in London at the Red Cross for a night out together. He stopped telling Jimmy the nagging problems going on at the base, and was taking his own advice by going with the flow, and staying as loose as a goose.

Now he was serving an apprenticeship for his future career. He spent his spare time and the time while on leave at boxing tournaments. With his duties on the base, and the tournaments, it was exhausting. His military job, keeping tabs on aircraft inventories of the enormous quantity of equipment going in and out, wasn't easy. He kept a tight check on the stock and his records were always up to date in spite of his absences at tournaments. Angelo felt if he was doing a job he had to give it his best.

During one of the tournaments being held in Ruislip, a few miles from London, he and Jimmy bought a couple of books on boxing at Foyle's, the famous London book store, as they wanted to learn more about the sport. As Pop had often told them, 'If a job is worth doing, do it properly!'

At one of the tournaments, after the fights and just before they were about to leave, a well set, handsome man in a Canadian uniform came over to introduce himself. His name was Eddie Borden and he was a friend of Chris Dundee. He had a warm and friendly personality, and they arranged to meet for drinks the next time they were together in London.

Angelo met Eddie a few times for drinks and talked mainly about boxing, never realizing that Eddie would turn out to be a valuable contact. A few years after their first meeting, Eddie had a conversation with Chris Dundee in New York that would be instrumental in changing Angelo's life. Eddie suggested that Chris use his youngest brother in his business. 'You couldn't do better than to use your own flesh and blood. Angelo is a nice kid. Give him a chance. He'll do okay.'

CHAPTER 4

1945 and bad news

1945 began with bad news. On 8 January, Philomena Mirenda had a
fatal accident. She was hit by an automobile while shopping. The Air
Corp, under the auspices of the Red Cross, gave the two heartbroken
brothers a temporary leave of absence, so they could be together for
the funeral. Angelo blamed himself for her death because he hadn't
been there. He hadn't had a real reason to the join the Army Air
Corp. He could have stayed at home in South Philadelphia and
become an ensign in the Navy. For weeks, he tormented himself with
the question 'Why? Why hadn't he stayed at home?'

The war continued relentlessly, however, and Angelo reported
back to his unit in Newbury. In February, Jimmy was posted to St
Quentin, France, and the following month, Angelo was made Staff
Sergeant, an achievement of which he was justly proud. He believed
he had worked hard for it and the news of his promotion was
uplifting, but he was not in the mood for a celebration. Shortly
afterwards he, too, was posted to France to a small town called
Amiens, about 45 miles west of St Quentin. He couldn't wait to tell
Jimmy about his promotion and that there were now two Sergeant

Dundees. Forty-five miles was nothing. He knew he'd get a chance to meet up with his brother Jimmy. It came sooner than he expected. Shortly after arriving in Amiens, he was called to Paris to a major ETO boxing tournament, and of course, Jimmy, would be working the corner with him.

This was a special tournament. After the service contests, Marcel Cerdan, the famous French middleweight was boxing an exhibition bout. These exhibition matches gave servicemen the opportunity to see some of the world's greatest fighters. Earlier in the year, in England, Angelo had watched the heavyweight champion of the world, Joe Louis box an exhibition. 'The Brown Bomber' was an idol of Angelo's and it was an enormous thrill, one he would never forget, to actually meet the champion and shake his hand. Over the years, Angelo and Joe had got to know each other and had become good friends. They shared a similar sense of humour, and an acute weakness for gambling.

* * *

As soon as the service contests were over in the Marcel Cerdan exhibition fight began, the Dundee boys quickly found a space at the back of the crowded hall where they could watch the talented, French-Algerian fighter. Before the Nazis occupied France, Marcel had been their national champion so the overwhelming welcome Marcel received from the Free French Forces was understandable.

After Marcel finished his exhibition fight, showered and changed, he and Jimmy had a short conversation in French. Jimmy, a bright young man, had learned the language from a French girlfriend he had met in St Quentin. Jimmy believed the only way to learn a foreign language was in bed with a beautiful woman. Whether

Jimmy gave Marcel some tips on American women, or some advice on American fighters will never be known, but the result was Marcel became a world champion in 1948 by beating Tony Zale. The following year he lost the title to the irrepressible Jake LaMotta. Marcel's boxing career and his life came to a tragic end on 27 October 1949 when he died in an aeroplane crash. Marcel was only an acquaintance, but when Angelo and Jimmy heard the news they felt as if they had lost a friend.

Many things were beginning to mould Angelo's character that would prepare him to succeed in his later career. Being made Staff Sergeant was a lot different from being a dogface GI. Now he had authority and was learning how to take charge. He often had ideas and plans and would want to talk them over with someone. Jimmy was only 45 miles away in St Quentin and getting to him shouldn't be an insurmountable problem, he thought. So one afternoon, with some spare time on his hands, Angelo decided to visit his brother. There happened to be an empty Jeep outside his office. Without a second thought, he jumped in and revved up the engine. As he pulled away, he called over to a corporal who was about to enter his office. 'Which way to St Quentin?'

'Turn right at the Base entrance and straight on. Turn left when you hit Iussy,' came the reply. With a roar of the engine, and a couple of false starts, the Jeep set off. When he arrived at Jimmy's quarters after an effortless 45-mile drive in second gear, his brother couldn't believe his eyes. Visibly shocked, Jimmy asked, 'What the hell are you doing in that Jeep? You can't drive.'

Angelo grinned, 'I know that. You know that, but this friggin' Jeep don't know that.'

They both got drunk that night and sat talking for hours. The discussion was serious and profound, though neither one of them remembered what it was about when they woke up the next morning. Angelo had to face the problem of driving back, and the bigger problem of explaining the absence of both himself and the Jeep. He decided to worry about it when he got there. After a 10-minute lesson from Jimmy on how to drive, Angelo set off. Back at the base no one seemed to notice that the Jeep or Angelo had been missing, and if they did, nobody said anything.

There was a lot of talk of Germany collapsing, but Allied soldiers were still being killed, and Angelo felt he would like to be a little closer to the fighting. Using some of his connections, he arranged to go on a few combat flights. He took off in a C47 cargo plane from an air base in Belgium to drop packs to forces at the front. The plane went in low and he pushed out the Para-packs and watched them float down to the ground. The soldiers on the ground waved, and Angelo waved back wildly, feeling part of the team. It was a great feeling. On the third flight, as they came in over their given position, Angelo was about to push out the Para-packs, but something made him hesitate. The guys on the ground hadn't returned his wave, which was unusual, and Angelo, in that split second, knew something was wrong. As he edged carefully forward in the cargo hold, trying to get a better look at the ground, machine-gun bullets ripped through the air towards him. He pulled back quickly as a bullet chipped away a piece of the unloading hatch. Another quick peep below confirmed that they were under attack by German soldiers. He got the hatch closed before you could say Adolf Hitler, and the pilot hightailed it back to the base.

One positive result of his flight was that it gave Angelo 'points', and these would help speed up his discharge from the military when the war ended. The cessation of hostilities came around quicker than most of the guys had expected. About eight weeks after Angelo's nerve-shattering flight over enemy lines, the Third Reich surrendered and, on 8 May 1945, the war in Europe was over.

Angelo saw out his time in Erlangen, Germany, where he drank beer and waited to go home. Early in 1946, Staff Sergeant Angelo Mirenda, who had not fired a shot at an enemy, was shipped home. Once again he became plain Angelo Mirenda.

CHAPTER 5

South Philly – a long way from the Big Apple

Back home in South Philly Angelo worked at the navy yard as an aircraft maintenance inspector and lived at home, and things seemed to be the same. But they were not. What had changed? Angelo realised it was he who was different. Living in the house on Morris Street brought back many memories of his mother, reopening the thinly covered emotional scars. Sometimes at night, he would lie awake in bed wondering if he would ever get over the grief. A year passed slowly but surely and the pain began to fade.

Angelo wasn't settled in his job. Before he left for the war, he had been working on prop-engine planes, but now all that had changed. This was the age of jet engines, advanced technology. It was complicated, and Angelo managed to get by, but anything more advanced baffled him. He knew how things worked, but he didn't know why. He read the blueprints, checked the electric cables, receptacle to receptacle. He worked on a giant switchboard but he had no overall picture of what was going on. He was out of his depth. The management offered to sign him up for a course on electronics, telling him that with his past record, it should be a cinch. Nevertheless, Angelo had learned to face up to his shortcomings. To take the course would mean five years of hard studying to master something he had no real passion for. He was honest enough to realise that after the discipline of his life in the services he really wanted to have some fun, and except for the minor pressure of his job, he *was* having fun. Most week nights were spent at the local dance hall. Weekends were for dancing in Atlantic City with his pals – and of course there were the girls. In many ways, it was like pre-war for him. No responsibilities, just having a ball. There were so many guys from South Philly having fun in Atlantic City, on the weekends they called the place South Philly on the Sea.

As he was spending so much of his time with his buddies, he didn't have time to miss seeing Jimmy, who was busy getting on with his own life. Without a word to anyone in the family, Jimmy had quietly gotten married. His bride was a lovely lady by the name of Louise who had sometimes been one of Angelo's dancing partners.

When Jimmy finally let the family know, there was no fuss – just congratulations, a handshake, a quick hug and a glass of vino. Salud! Angelo was very happy for Jimmy and Louise and thought it typical of Jimmy. Angelo thought he would do it that way too, when he found the right girl.

Still, dissatisfaction with his life nagged at Angelo. It wasn't that it was bad, it was just okay, at best. The problems at work didn't help and the realization that he was getting nowhere at a rapid pace, and that this was going to be the rest of his life, working and living in South Philly, made him feel unsettled. In 1947, that fateful conversation was taking place in New York between Eddie Borden, the Canadian service man Angelo had met at an ETO tournament in England, and his elder brother Chris. The result of the conversation would change Angelo's life.

One afternoon after work, Angelo got home and heard his father talking on the phone. Pop was smiling. 'It's Chris,' he said, in his thick Italian accent, as he turned his head away from the phone for a moment, and then immediately resumed his conversation. After a minute or two, he handed the phone to Angelo. 'He wanna talk to you.' For reasons Angelo could never explain he felt fear and elation simultaneously. That feeling stayed with him after he had hung up the phone. Chris had asked him if he would like to go to New York and work for him. Angelo didn't even have to think about it. 'Sure Chris. Sounds good. When do you want me?'

Angelo came from a big city and had travelled widely through Europe and England, but when Angelo arrived in New York, he was bowled over. Maybe it was because he was going to live and work in the Big Apple – and not some nice suburb on the outskirts of the City but the heart of Manhattan. That's where the action was. Right there, just opposite the world famous Madison Square Garden, known everywhere as the Garden. No wonder he was in awe.

As soon as he arrived in New York, he made his way to the Capitol Hotel, his new home. It would have been good to have spent a day or two getting the feel of the place before going to work, whatever that was going to be, but brother Chris believed in that old adage, 'Waste not, want not.'

That night, Chris had Angelo assisting in the corner for one of his fighters at the Garden. In between rounds, Angelo, who was so scared it was difficult to concentrate, would quickly put his bucket up into the ring, positioned so the corner men could reach it easily and the fighter spit out his water mouthwash into it. Angelo had done bucket work before, but that night at the Garden was something else. The one-minute break between rounds seemed like 10 seconds. Everything happened so fast. He was one step away from panic. 'Where's Jimmy when I need him?' he thought to himself.

That night, after his New York debut, Angelo didn't hang around. He was too tired both physically and mentally. He grabbed a sandwich and coffee from a deli, and went back to the hotel, where he fell asleep listening to the radio.

Chris's office was a room in the hotel, Room 711, and Angelo lived and worked there. It had a studio bed at one end and two desks at the other, a wash basin and a shower. Angelo felt that, no matter what happened, at least he'd have somewhere to sleep. Each morning after he had made the bed into a couch once again, it looked like an office. After army life, Angelo had no problems with it and settled in quickly.

On fight night, he worked the corner. Each time it became a little easier and his nervousness slowly disappeared. After the fights, he would go out with the boys. As the youngest in the group, he liked to hang out with sports writers, trainers and corner men who were established in their profession. Most nights, when they talked about boxing, he kept his mouth shut and listened, always learning. One thing he couldn't get the hang of was how Chris did business. Angelo thought Chris handled about 12 fighters, but with Chris you never knew. His left hand didn't know what his right hand was doing. Chris made so many different arrangements with various managers and fighters it took Angelo a long time to understand it.

Some mornings, Angelo typed up promotional material on all the fighters. It was one of Angelo's duties to type the fighter's records and statistics on the back of their photographs. It was pretty basic. He would then send the photograph with a covering letter giving the fighter's personal background – 'He is good to his mother and goes to church every Sunday' – not exactly heavy stuff – to sports writers in the cities where the fighters were scheduled to appear. Sometimes, the fighter would get a human interest piece written about him. When a fighter got a mention it was good publicity – publicity meant interest and interest meant bigger gates. Bigger gates meant bigger paydays for the fighter, and more money for the fighter meant more money for the fighter's manager. It was something Chris latched on to early. Angelo soaked up that knowledge, developing a promotion and publicity 'know how' he would use in later life when he represented fighters.

Chris normally arrived at the office around 10.30am. Without a smile he would say, 'Hi kid, any calls?' He'd walk over to the desk, flick his hat onto the couch, 'Where are my messages? I gotta make a call.' Angelo never bothered to answer him, because Chris was already on the phone. He would give Chris the mail and the pad with his phone messages written on it, and get back to typing the backs of photographs.

The 15-year difference in their ages made their relationship difficult sometimes. To Chris, Angelo was the kid brother he hardly knew. Now, he was giving the kid a chance. To Angelo, Chris was the brother who had sent him boxing gloves as a kid. He was a 'big time' manager of fighters, a 'somebody'. But first and foremost, he was still his brother and Angelo loved him.

It didn't take him long to learn that Chris was hardworking and clever and Angelo admired him. Chris had a fancy address in Long Beach, Long Island. He had turned a nickel and dime business into a respected and successful operation. Sometimes, he represented as many as 20 fighters. Everybody seemed to know Chris. Not bad for an Italian kid who had left his home in South Philly at 15 years of age. How could young Angelo not admire a brother like that?

Angelo didn't quit his old job, but had taken a leave of absence. He was too unsure of what the future would hold for him. It had crossed his mind that he might have to return to Philly and it was reassuring to know he would have a comfortable safety net to fall into if things didn't work out. Angelo knew he hadn't been Chris's first choice for the job. Chris had originally wanted Jimmy, but Jimmy had just got married to Louise, and the job was too intangible and precarious for a married man. Angelo knew that if he didn't do a good job Chris would find somebody else.

In the short time Angelo had been in New York, he made up his mind about two things: (1) He didn't want to go back to South Philly to his job as a maintenance inspector; (2) He did want to do something that involved the fight game. Right now, he was only the bucket boy, but he did it well. He was learning what needed to be done when working the corner.

Angelo got on well with fighters. They could be temperamental at times, like many highly trained artists and athletes. But, after training sessions, or after the fights at the Garden, Angelo would sit around and socialise with them. No heavy stuff. Maybe they would re-live a fight, talk about what they should have done, or just everyday things, with a few laughs thrown in. They would tell jokes. And to this day, Angie loves a good joke.

It didn't go unnoticed that Angelo was a talented kid. Chickie Ferrara, the trainer, stopped him one day. 'Hey, Angie, I've been watching you. You got a nice way with the fighters. They like and respect you. Stay in the game. You gotta feeling for it. If you need any help, all you gotta do is ask.' Angelo was embarrassed but flattered because Chickie was one of boxing's most respected trainers. Being respected was very important in the boxing fraternity. Someday, Angelo hoped he'd be as respected as Chickie, and perhaps even as much as Chris was.

Angelo had seen how the out of town managers respected Chris. Chris would arrange for their fighters to get a bout in New York, and maybe, even at the Garden. That was clout. When Chris was working out a deal he could be charming or aggressive. He could certainly negotiate. One of the mangers told Angelo that Chris had more moves than a chessboard. Not everyone liked him, but they couldn't help but respect him.

The highlight of Angelo's day was going to Stillman's Gym to watch the fighters work out. Stillman's was to boxers what Harvard Law School is to lawyers. It was a place of training and learning. It was a school with any number of famous alumni. The fighters competed against their peers under the scrutiny and tutelage of astute and knowledgeable coaches. Attending the place didn't guarantee success, but it certainly helped. Angelo stayed in the background, he listened, watched and absorbed the knowledge. As Angelo climbed the well worn stairs of Stillman's Gym, the smell of sweat and liniment oil filled his nostrils. The buzzing of voices mingled with the thump of a heavy punching bag, and he could hear the staccato rap of a speed-bag being hit, partnered by the monotonous whine of a skipping-rope. It was like a symphony to him and Angelo loved it.

He saw many big name fighters at Stillman's, like Rocky Graziano who was great to watch during sparring sessions. Angelo also met famous managers and trainers. When Al Weill, once manager of former lightweight champion, Lou Ambers, gave him a nod, Angelo was thrilled. He met Charlie Goldman, an experienced fight manager, who became the trainer and manager of legend Rocky Marciano, at Stillman's Gym. Goldman befriended him, recognizing his love and aptitude for the fight game. He also warned Angelo against betting on a fight in which he was working. He often gave the young Angelo the sort of sound advice he would never forget.

'If you bet on your own guy, your judgment could be influenced,' said Goldman. 'Thinking about the money instead of the fighter could cause you to lose the detached, analytical approach. You might exert too much pressure on the fighter by worrying too much about losing. Needless to say, if you had big buck on the other fighter there would always be the temptation to ruin or damage your own guy's chances.' Angelo never bet on a fight in which he was involved.

Angelo went to Stillman's everyday of the week, except for national holidays when the gym was closed. His duties for Chris included being available at the weigh-in and press conference. It had been a great thrill for him when Chris first took him to the Garden for a press conference. It made him feel like part of the team and proud to be Chris's brother. Chris was not easy to get along with though he could certainly turn on the charm. He was particularly touchy about giving away fight tickets to the many people who wanted them, usually for nothing. Apart from a few people, especially those doing current business with him, Chris told them

straight, 'You wanna ticket? Go across to the Garden and buy one.'
If they offered to buy one, but pay Chris later, he would say, 'What
am I, a bookkeeper?' Chris was tough but it was a tough business.

In 1948 professional boxing was going through changes, many
badly needed. It wasn't just New York that had problems. It was a
nationwide ailment. On 20 February, in Illinois, a boxer by the
name of Sammy Baroudi died after his fight. There was an outcry
for pre-fight medical examinations. Another boxer, T. Harmon
from Massachusetts, collapsed after excessive weight reduction and
his licence was revoked.

Boxing was getting organised, and positive action was being
taken. In New York, Abe Greene was elected the first Commissioner
by the NBA (National Boxing Association) and Edward Eagan was
confirmed as Athletic Commissioner. It became mandatory for
boxers to have a medical examination before a fight. It became a rule
that a fighter must report any injuries before a fight. The famous
middleweight, Jake LaMotta, found himself under investigation for
not reporting an injury. Sixty-six boxers were found unfit to fight
and had their licences revoked, a ruling that probably saved more
than one boxer's life.

There were inquiries and investigations into crime and
monopolies in boxing. Newspaper headlines had screamed of
bribery and corruption. Now something was being done about it.
There was a strong faction that wanted to stop professional boxing
altogether on the grounds it was too violent. Sportsmen died while
playing baseball, football, skiing or ice hockey, but that never made
the headlines. Boxing was stigmatised, yet it was a sport that did a
great deal of good getting violent kids off the streets and channelling
their energy safely.

Angelo was naturally aware that there were crooks and gangsters in the game, as there were in most New York businesses, but fight-fixing happened rarely. Angelo never experienced it until one night, at the Whiteplains Country Center, he was working as Ray Arcel's assistant in the corner for Bill Bossio, one of Chris's up and coming young fighters. Bill, a slick featherweight, had won a few fights around the New York area and was popular at the Country Center. The bookmakers had made him a four-to-one favourite.

Ray Arcel, the trainer and corner man for Bossio, didn't need Angelo hanging around the overcrowded changing room, so Angelo took the opportunity to catch a fight in progress. He stood at the back of the hall getting acclimatised. Bossio's fight was coming up next. He was so engrossed in the fight that he didn't notice the two guys who strolled over and stood next to him. The bell sounded for the end of the round. Angelo turned and looked at the two men. One was about 40 with black, curly hair. Angelo had seen him before at other fights. The other guy, who was young, slim and hard-looking, smiled at him and leaned close. 'What do you think of Bossio's chance?'

'Great. He'll probably stop the other guy,' Angelo answered loudly to overcome the noisy crowd.

'Yeah, you're probably right, but if Bossio doesn't win, a hundred bucks on the other guy at four-to-one, would net you four big ones.' He leaned in closer and whispered into Angelo's ear. 'I'll put the bet on for you. It'll cost you nothin'. Listen to me, Angelo, if you do us a little favour, I'll pay you your winnings right here and now. Four hundred bucks.'

Angelo might have been naïve, but he was no dummy. He knew a bribe when he heard one. Some of the guys that hung around

Stillman's Gym had told him that it went on. He just didn't think that anyone would ever be stupid enough to try and bribe him. The hard-looking guy persisted. He spoke very persuasively. 'Listen, kid, all you gotta do is drop somethin' on the sponge in round four. And when you wipe his face in between rounds, just make sure he gets some of this in his eyes.' He held a small jar of salve between his thumb and forefinger. He gave Angelo a confidential smirk and continued, 'Just make certain he gets it in his eyes. And just for doing that little thing, you get this.' He handed the salve to Curly Hair, then took a roll of bills from his pocket and slowly peeled off four one-hundred dollar bills and pushed them towards Angelo.

The bell went for the next round, but Angelo had lost all interest in watching the fight. He was steaming, and had a problem controlling his voice. His anger must have shown. 'Look pal, I'm not interested. I don't bet.' He said as he pushed the curly–headed guy out of his way and went to walk past.

'Hold it, punk. We ain't finished with you yet,' Curly Hair snarled.

'Yes, you are.' Angelo threw a short hard left to his belly, and the guy gasped for air and doubled up. Angelo could easily have thrown a right–hand punch and really hurt him, but common sense prevailed. There was no point in making a scene and an enemy too. For a moment, he stood there staring hard at the two guys, then turned his back on them and quickly walked back to the dressing room.

Ray Arcel gave Angelo a quick look when he entered, but said nothing. Angelo leaned against a wall and stood quietly and unobtrusively until it was time to make their way down to the ring. From the ring Angelo scanned the crowd looking for the two guys.

There was no sign of them. He felt a little easier. When the fight started, his concentration obliterated everything else from his mind except the job at hand. The fight was short and successful. Bill Bossio won with a knockout in the third round.

Later, after Bill had changed and it was time to leave the Whiteplains Country Center, Angelo felt a wave of apprehension wash over him. Would the two guys be waiting for him? The Bossio entourage left through the back door. Angelo kept close to Ray Arcel. He looked up and down the parking lot, but there was no one hanging around. Relieved, he got into the car. The drive back to Manhattan was mostly quiet. Angelo would never forget that evening.

The incident played on his mind. Had they really been trying to bribe him, or just testing to see if he could be bought? No, it was a bribe, all right. Over the next couple of months, Angelo saw the curly-haired guy a couple of times, but they never spoke. Angelo became cautious when leaving an arena, always expecting someone to be waiting for him outside for revenge. A few years passed before they spoke again. Angelo was in Chicago working with Carmen Basilio. Like their first meeting, Angelo was standing at the back of the arena, watching a fight. This time, he was not alone. He was standing with one of the sports writers from the *Chicago Tribune*. Curly Hair was talking to his hard-faced buddy. As they walked by, they recognised Angelo, and gave him a friendly wave. Curly Hair said, 'Hi Angie. How ya doin'?' Angelo just nodded.

'Do you know those guys?' the newspaperman asked.

'No. Not really, I've seen them around. Do you know them?' Angelo asked.

'Sorta. They're a couple of wise guys. The little guy is Johnny

Gold. I read a story about him recently. He knifed a guy. Cut him up pretty bad. I'm surprised he's not in jail.' Angelo nodded but didn't say a word. He was too busy wondering if the friendly wave had sinister undertones. Were they still out to get him? Fortunately, he never found out because he never saw the two guys again. And no one ever tried to bribe Angelo again.

CHAPTER 6

Working for Chris

Things were changing in 1948. A new phenomenon, television, had invaded the fight game. It would bring in much needed revenue but it was also creating problems. The Twentieth Century Sporting Club, Inc., an important promotional company, was in conflict with the Managers' Guild over the television rights for the big New York venues, the Madison Square Garden and the St Nicholas Arena. A boycott was put into operation, but after a short time the argument was settled. The Guild ended up receiving 50 per cent of telecast rights at the two venues. It was an exciting time to be in New York, and Angelo was finding his excitement at the Garden on fight nights and at Stillman's Gym every day. There was always something new to see, hear, or learn. Angelo was learning the tricks of the trade from the best in the business.

Charlie Goldman, now Angelo's friend and mentor, a five-foot-one bundle of energy, had been 60 years young when they first met in Stillman's Gym. They used to go out for coffee after the fights, and Charlie always had some wise words, even if at first they sounded a little unusual. 'If you get a good idea for your fighter, like a different move or somethin', tell your fighter in a way that will make him believe he really thought of it himself. Understood? You see, that way, he'll make the move naturally, without worrying about if he's doing it right. Plant the seeds, plant the seeds. You know what I'm saying?' He made a lot of sense, and later in his career, Angelo would borrow that advice when working with a boxer by the name of Cassius Clay.

Chris's boxers were now being sent out of the State of New York to fight. He used various trainers to work with them. Chickie Ferrara looked after five. It was usual for the trainer to go out of town with the fighter and work the corner too. Chris told Angelo he could go out on the road with the fighters as he was ready to handle it. It would be his first time dealing with the business side, and it was going to be his first time as 'boss' in the corner, even though he was the only guy working there. There was a lot about it Angelo didn't know, but he was excited about giving it a try. The better paid fighters would use two or even three corner men, but the less well-known fighters could only afford one guy. That guy had to be able to do everything. Working in the New York area was a breeze, as Chris would always be there to handle the business side of things, but on the road it was a different ball game. Someone had to deal with the promoter, make certain the correct purse was picked up without any last-minute invented deductions – tricks like that did happen. As a corner man, Angelo would have to check out the medication needed for cuts, bruises and swellings, as well as making sure he had smelling salts, bandages, vaseline and other requirements like scissors, gloves, shorts, robes, protectors and the boxer's wardrobe. He was going to be paid $15 for the night, which put pressure on him. Chris was going to pay him to handle everything on his own and giving it a try and failing was better than not trying at all.

Chris supplied a car and a driver, a guy by the name of Dick Vick. Angelo would arrange the 'meet' with the fighter, depending on where he lived and where they were going. Dick would pick them up and set off to the venue. On his first time out as 'boss' it all went smoothly, and his fighter won. It continued that way, not that his fighters always won, but he had no problems. It wasn't until years later, when he worked with Carmen Basilio, that he realised just how amateurish he must have been. It takes time and experience to gain the confidence needed to act with speed and certainty when your fighter is cut and hurt, to be able to read a fight, know how to motivate your fighter, fully understand what your fighter needs to do and to be sufficiently knowledgeable to know if your fighter can do it. Like most sports that have demanding disciplines and a high level of skill, becoming a master at it is a big achievement. A wise athlete understands that no matter how good he or she gets in their chosen field, they never know it all, and the learning goes on forever. One day, Angelo would become a master, but he would always be learning.

That first week, after settling up with Chris, and paying the fighter, Angelo earned $45 dollars from his out-of-town corner work. However, when it came to getting paid for his office work, that was a different story. Payday came around but Chris didn't pay him. Angelo didn't say anything as he figured Chris would pay him later. Another Friday came along, and then another Friday went by, and he still had not been paid. He still didn't say anything. Angelo was embarrassed about it. After all, he was being paid for his out-of-town fights. It was his office work he hadn't been paid for. The amount he was owed was negligible, but he felt he should have been paid. Angelo thought about it but decided not to rock the boat. He never mentioned the wages. It was because he enjoyed going on the road with the fighters – he felt like he was being useful, and he knew he was doing a good job – and being the guy in charge made the wages situation a bit more bearable. Angelo was juiced up about Bob Isler's next out-of-town fight. On paper it looked a good fight. Saint Paul, a fighter who was a local favourite, was going against Angelo's guy, Bob Isler. It turned out to be a tough fight but ended in a win for Isler. The small crowd was ecstatic, but that was no consolation for Angelo as he did his best to patch up his fighter. For the first time as a corner man he was painfully aware of his inexperience and inadequacies. Was he treating the cut above Bob's left eye correctly? And the right eye was so bruised it was closing. What should he do? What would Ray Arcel do? Bob was taking a beating and Angelo was at a loss to find the right words of advice. All he could do was his best and he did, but Angelo was far from satisfied with himself.

Angelo collected the purse from the promoter, who was happy with the fight. In the dressing room, Angelo deducted Chris's expenses, put his money in an envelope to give to him in the morning, and gave the other two-thirds of the money to Bob.

'Hey Angie, you ain't taken your cut,' Bob mumbled through cut and swollen lips. Angelo looked at his bruised, scarred face. 'Forget it, Bob. This one's on me.' He turned away and began packing his bag.

Strangely, the drive back was fun. Dick Vick, a happy guy, although a little weird, would never put his dashboard lights on so at night the interior of the car would be in total darkness. He would tell the latest jokes he had picked up from his Broadway pals, Bob cracked a few gags, and Angelo told the stories he had heard at Stillman's. They had plenty of laughs and the mauling and beating of an hour ago was forgotten.

Working for Chris, except for the lack of paychecks, was exciting and enjoyable as there was always something new to learn, even if Chris wasn't easy to deal with. Chris learned early to make his own decisions. When as a young man he met Geraldine, the girl he loved, he married her. It made no difference to him that she was Jewish and he was a Catholic. Angelo had agreed with his brother's decision, and now he had met a girl who had turned his thoughts to marriage. She wasn't Catholic or Jewish – she was a Southern Methodist. Dundee wasn't sure about the differences. He had no problems with any religion as long as it didn't interfere with his life. As far as he was concerned, God bless them all. Meanwhile, his top priority was to earn a living in the fight game. To get married, you needed a few dollars in your pocket. Some in the bank would be good too!

Helen Bolton, the name of the young lady in question, was from Georgia and was working as a model in New York. Her cousin was Jack Cranford, a well-known heavyweight who was handled by Chris Dundee and trained by Ray Arcel, so it was no surprise that they met. After a few casual meetings at the Garden, where Helen often went to see the fights, they began dating. They became regulars at Toots Shor's and Jack Dempsey's, two of the most popular New York nightspots for showbiz and sports celebrities. Angelo loved going there. The problem was paying for it. Helen was making good money as a model and without too much argument from Angelo, she sometimes picked up the tab. Whatever his thoughts were on marriage, they had to be put on hold. Money was a constant worry. It was not the right time to ask Chris for more, as he was having business problems. Angelo tried to be positive, but a nasty feeling about the future was eating away at him.

* * *

Joe Louis, a great role model for boxing, retired from fighting on 1 May 1949. In the 1970s, Joe was working as a host in Caesar's Palace in Las Vegas. It was a perfect job for him as he loved people and he always had the time and patience to sign autographs for his many fans. Unfortunately, Joe was in the ideal job but in the wrong place. The gambling temptations in Vegas were too much, and over the years Joe dropped a lot of money. Angelo was a constant visitor to Caesar's, and never failed to lose at the tables. Losing money became a habit, a habit he shared with Louis.

On one occasion in the late seventies, Dundee was in Las Vegas, or as he sometimes calls it, 'Lost Wages', and got a bad attack of the gambling bug. He sat at the table, watching his chips disappear, trying to control that particular feeling of panic when you're dropping a stack of money that is more than you can afford to lose. One of the casino managers came over to him, placed a friendly arm on his shoulder, and asked very politely if he could have a quick, few words with him. Angelo looked up at the manager's smiling face and, hiding his sense of foreboding, replied, 'Of course.'

The casino manager immediately began to tell Dundee that his pal Joe Louis had lost a few big ones and would Angelo mind signing Joe's markers? The manager, with little subtlety, waved the pieces of paper in Dundee's face, who didn't know whether to laugh or cry. Like most people, the manager thought Angelo was earning millions of dollars with Muhammad Ali and naturally thought Angelo would be pleased to help out an old pal. Under normal circumstances there would have been no problem, but right there and then, Angelo was more than concerned about how he could cover his own losses.

He had no choice other than to say, 'Tell Joe I can't make it right for him. I'm gonna have a problem settling my own account.' Angelo paused and gave the manager a helpless grin. 'Just say Angelo is having his usual run. He'll know what you mean. And yeah, tell him if he can give me a little time, I'll try and work somethin' out.'

Joe Louis did understand. He had watched Dundee lose nearly every time he played. On that particular night, when he and Dundee met up later at the bar, Louis laughed off his own and Angelo's bad night. 'You know, Angelo, you and craps just don't get along.'

From that night on Louis always called Angelo the 'magician'. Joe Louis would smile that sweet smile of his and said, 'When you gamble, Angelo, you do one hell of a trick, you turn money into crap.'

Joe Louis's retirement left a vacant championship. Chris told Angelo weeks before it was officially announced that it would be Ezzard Charles against Jersey Joe Walcott for the title, and he was right. Unfortunately, the fight was going to be held in Chicago, not New York. Chris was not happy because he wanted the fight in New York for business reasons. He was making arrangements to go to Cincinnati for the Gus Lesvenich–Joey Maxim, light-heavyweight championship fight. 'Go round to the Forest Hotel, Angie, see Jack

Kearns and give him this envelope and pick up my tickets. Can you believe what's going on? Cincinnati gets Joey Maxim against Gus Lesvenich, Detroit is getting Jake LaMotta against Marcel Cerdan, and Chicago the Charles–Walcott fight. New York is getting zilch.'

Angelo made his way to the Forest Hotel, where many out-of-town fight people stayed. He'd often run this kind of errand for Chris and it gave him the opportunity to meet new people. At first, he was 'Chris's kid brother' but eventually they discovered that his name was Angelo.

Jack (Doc) Kearns had just flown in from Cincinnati, where his fighter, Joey Maxim, was preparing for the title shot. He was sitting in a bathrobe talking to a guy Angelo thought he knew from the New York Boxing Commission. Angelo gave Doc the envelope. Kearns, without bothering to open and check the contents, handed Angelo a similar-looking envelope. Reaching into the pocket of his bathrobe, he took out a roll of bills. He peeled off a 20 and gave it to Angelo for his trouble – what trouble! He left feeling good. In the elevator was a sharp, well-dressed guy that he was sure he had seen before.

'Hi, I'm Angelo Dundee. Don't I know you?'

'No,' he said, 'you don't, but I've heard of your brother, Chris. I'm Frankie Carbo.'

Frankie Carbo. Of course. Angelo has seen his picture in the Los Angeles papers and he had a great memory for faces. It was alleged that Carbo was a 'Mister Big' in organised crime. Angelo smiled back at him, trying not to stare. When the elevator stopped at the ground floor and the door opened, Carbo gave Angelo a nod and strode off. Neither knew their paths would cross again.

Chris was always telling Angelo what to do. How to handle this, how to handle that. Invariably, the instructions were on the button. One day in the office, Angelo was paying one of the fighters for the previous night's fight. The guy took his money. 'Angie,' he said, 'OK if I settle with you after the next fight? I gotta lot of problems at home right now.' Chris looked at Angelo.

'Sure, no problem,' Angie said. After the fighter had left Chris pointed his finger in Angie's direction and began laying into him.

'What the hell are you doing? You wanna end up broke? What are you, some kind of bank or something? If you wanna go into the loan business, I'll introduce you to some of the boys. You know these kids ain't going to pay you back. You ain't a charitable organization, are you?' Angelo shrugged his shoulders. What could he say? But Chris wasn't finished with him yet. 'Angelo, you gotta say no. Tell them you ain't got it and I'll tell you something for nothing – you ain't got it.'

Charlie Goldman called Angelo later that day. He told him that Rocky Marciano had four straight KOs, and none of them had lasted longer than five rounds. Rocky was still fighting out of Brockton, Massachusetts, and Charlie gave Angelo an open invitation to come over to see Rocky fight. He wished them both luck and got back to the day's work – he wanted to clear his desk and have a worry-free weekend.

A worry-free weekend! That was a laugh. Angelo had made arrangements with Helen to drive down to Salisbury, North Carolina, to meet her parents – he had been worrying about it all week. Still, he knew he couldn't back out and he wouldn't want to disappoint Helen. Maybe it would work out just fine.

That night, after the usual fights, Helen went home to pack for the trip and Angelo hung around the Garden where Al Buck, of the

New York Post, ran into him and invited him to go for a drink at Dempsey's bar. They settled in and talked about who they thought would be the next heavyweight champion, Charles or Walcott, and they both went for Jersey Joe. After their second round of whiskeys, Jack Dempsey joined them at the bar. Angelo casually mentioned that he was going to North Carolina with Helen in the morning. Al said that it sounded like a cue for a song. Jack looked at Angelo for a moment. 'Angie, I know you and Helen have been going out quite a while now…' He hesitated. Angelo was getting worried. 'Hey kid, don't get worried. What I want to say is that I got Helen's phone number from Gerri Marrott, you know, Helen's friend, who used to be quite a regular, I gave Helen a call and asked her over for supper. Hey, cut it out will you,' he said, seeing Angelo's chin hit his chest. 'This was all before she met you, you dummy. Would I try and cut in on a buddy?' The relief flooded over Angelo.

'Anyway,' Jack continued, 'she came over, and would you believe this, she brought Gerri along too. We had supper – the three of us – and that, brother, was that. I'm only telling you 'cause I want you to know what a great lady you got there. She's a nice kid. Take care of her.'

Angelo beamed at him. 'You bet your life, Jack. North Carolina, here I come.'

The romantic side of Angelo's life was blooming, which was good because it took his mind off the business side, which was withering. He didn't know the full story, however, because Chris kept things to himself. One morning, Chris arrived at the office, as usual, around 10.30. Angelo handed him the mail. 'What's that?' he asked Chris, indicating a large buff-coloured envelope displaying in large bold print the name of an insurance company. Chris stared at it, then began tapping his desktop with one of the pointed corners of the envelope.

'Why don't you open it?' The repetitive tap was getting on Angelo's nerves.

'You know that Fort Hamilton and Sunnyside have dried up, don't you?' He was talking about two halls where boxing matches were held. Angie had heard about their closing down. He wondered what the envelope had to do with it.

'Look kid,' Chris didn't look happy and his voice was tired, 'things ain't going so good. That's another two venues gone, and there ain't hardly anything around here any more. You'll be lucky if you work twice this week, and let me tell you, the out-of-town deals don't make me enough to pay the phone bill. Do you hear what I'm saying?' Angelo heard all right. 'You see this?' He waved the envelope at Angelo's face. 'This is my insurance course application. Yeah, that's right.' He went on to answer the question forming in Angie's mind. 'I'm gonna take an insurance course. I'm gonna sell insurance. I gotta make a living and I hear this is a good racket.'

Angelo could only stare at Chris. He didn't know what to say. What was he telling him? Were we going to close down? Angie knew one thing for sure, there was no way he was going to be an insurance salesman. No offence to the profession, but it wasn't in the cards for Angelo, and he couldn't really see Chris doing it either. He would have to wait and see what happened. For the next few months the office remained open, and they managed to arrange bouts for their reduced stable of fighters. He worked enough to keep his head above water – just. Helen understood, and didn't worry about not going to expensive places. She had only known Angelo broke, so he guessed she hardly noticed the difference.

In the back of his mind was a feeling of anxiety. He tried to keep it suppressed, but at lonely moments – and he had many – a feeling of impending doom would surface and he had a tough fight to keep it from taking over. He noticed that Chris and his wife, Geraldine, and even Helen, in some unguarded moments, seemed worried. He guessed it was the uncertainty of everything, which he knew could be worse than facing the facts, but he did his best to bury his fears.

Chris, as usual, was hustling and bustling, yet he still found time to study his insurance course. Each day Angelo wondered if Chris would say that he was closing the office, leaving him on his own. He had no plans for that eventuality.

CHAPTER 7

'Good luck, kid   I'll be in touch'

Angelo had been at Stillman's Gym, working with Bill Bossio. After the workout, Bill and he swapped a few stories and had a laugh. Angelo liked the kid and hoped that he would do well. He gave him the arrangements for the following night's fight, and made him write down the time of the pickup. That way, if he was late, he couldn't say that Angelo had made a mistake over the time. Although Bill wasn't like that, a few of the guys were. They had an answer for everything, so Angelo began making them write down all the arrangements. Some of those characters still lost the piece of paper.

Angelo made his way to the Garden cafeteria to see who was hanging around. He had no plans for the afternoon and, as far as he knew, Chris was out of town in Miami. He saw Joe Cernoff, a good friend of Chris's, drinking a coffee. Maybe Joe might have a bright idea how to kill the rest of the day. He might also know something about Chris's trip to Miami. He had been talking to some guys there on the phone for the past four or five weeks and he had gone south to the Sunshine State to check something out. Angelo was hazy about the proposition as Chris always kept things to himself. Nevertheless, Angelo was excited and confident that if there was a deal floating around, Chris would nail it down. Wouldn't it be great if there was going to be some action in Miami – he could get a tan too!

Joe looked up when Angelo reached his table. 'Don't sit down,' he said. 'Chris is looking for you. He said for you to go straight to the office. He must have missed you at Stillman's.' So Chris was back. However, at the office, he broke the news that he was selling his home on Long Island and moving to Miami where he planned to promote fights. A venue had been set up on Miami Beach. Angelo could keep the office that was also his home. The rent was paid until the end of the month. If he wanted, he could have Bill Bossio to manage, and if things worked out in Florida, and he wasn't doing anything special, he could come down and join Chris and his wife, Geraldine.

'Good luck, kid. I'll be in touch,' said Chris, casually dismissing Angelo.

Fighting his way through the shock and panic, Angelo gradually felt a tingle of excitement seeping through. He had his own fighter, Bill Bossio. He was a manager. He would get by.

* * *

In one way, Helen was responsible for Angelo moving to Miami. During the summer of 1951, when he was working on his own in New York, Helen went to visit her Aunt Nora and Uncle John, who lived in Miami. While she was there she met up with Chris, who was promoting boxing on the beach. He was doing OK, and he suggested to Helen that Angelo could be of use if he came down. It was more a suggestion than a firm offer but when she returned to New York, Helen pursued the subject.

One evening, as they were having supper at the Stage Door Deli, Helen began telling Angelo about Miami Beach and what a wonderful place it was. 'You don't have to sell me on Miami,' he said. 'I loved it way back.'

'It was so hot when I drove down, I couldn't put the top down,' enthused Helen. 'Angie. Can you imagine, if you were working down there you could go swimming practically every day.'

The waiter arrived with the sandwiches. 'Do you want another beer, Angie?' Angelo was a regular and the waiter knew him.

'Yeah, bring another couple. Have you ever been to Miami Beach?' Angie asked him.

'Are you kidding? Me and the wife go every year. It's got more class than Atlantic City, and the weather's always good. I'll get the beers. Eat and enjoy.'

Helen smiled and started to attack her corned beef sandwich. 'I'll give Chris a call,' Angelo said.

Chris told him over the phone that if he came down to Miami he would find something for Angelo. He would get $75 a week. As it stood now, he wasn't making enough to save a dime, so he prepared to kiss goodbye to New York. He needed some stake money, and he knew where to place his hands on it. During his spell in the service, he had sent most of his pay home to Mom in South Philly. It had been for her personally, but she hadn't spent it. She had saved it for him. He made arrangements with the bank to withdraw a total sum of $1,200. The office/home at the hotel was paid for and his business was such that it took all of four hours to clear up everything. One problem was that he wasn't taking

Helen with him. When he got settled and could be sure that his job wouldn't evaporate, he would ask Helen to marry him. Would she say, 'Yes'? Another problem was what to do with Bill Bossio – in the end he was taken over by Al Braverman. It was arranged that Angelo would retain a small percentage as he had progressed Bill's fee up to $5,000 for a fight at the Garden. Al said he would send the money to Miami. That was October 1951 and it still hasn't arrived to this day.

He convinced fighters Bill Neri, who was a lightweight, and Alex Fimbres, who was a featherweight, to take a chance and come to Miami with him. They figured that even if things didn't work out, at least they'd get a good sun tan. They were fighting out of New York and living in Phoenix. They were nice kids and he hoped things would go well for them, though he could promise them nothing. They knew the fight game was tough and precarious, and they knew Angelo would do his best for them.

Angelo settled quickly into his new life on Miami Beach. He stayed in a hotel on 17th Street and Alton Road. It wasn't much of a place, but it was near the office, and it was an improvement on New York – at least he wasn't living in the office.

His first four months on Miami Beach breezed by effortlessly, and as far as working for Chris again was concerned, it was just like old times. The two main differences were that there was no Stillman's Gym, and that meant none of his pals was around, and he missed the hustle and bustle of Manhattan. However, he loved the clean, brightly painted art deco buildings and the clear blue sky of Miami Beach. He'd had this love affair with the area from the time he had first gone there in 1943 with the Air Corps. To be actually living there and earning a living should have made him feel great, but it didn't because he was lonely. He missed Helen. Angelo knew Miami was the place for him, and that really meant a place for Helen and him together. He realised he was thinking more about his impending marriage than about his two fighters.

However, before he could get married, he'd have to take a blood test. During the medical check–up that Chris had arranged, things took an unexpected turn. After the blood sample had been taken, Angelo remembered nothing until he heard the doctor asking, 'Do you feel all right, Angelo?'

'Sure, I feel OK,' Angelo answered. But he couldn't understand why he was stretched out on the sofa. 'What happened?' he asked, afraid to hear the answer.

'You fainted, son, when you saw the blood. Don't worry about it. This happens to a lot of people.'

'Well I gotta tell you, Doc, I shouldn't think too many cut men faint when they see blood, especially when it's their own.'

On Sunday, 11 February 1952, at noon, Helen Bolton and Angelo Dundee became husband and wife. They held the wedding ceremony at Chris's house. Judge Sapperstein officiated. The wedding was cosmopolitan, to say the least. A Philadelphia-Italian-Catholic guy and a Southern Methodist gal were married by a Jewish New Yorker who lived in Miami.

They rented an apartment on Miami Beach. When Angelo handed over the keys to Helen, he bowed and said grandly, 'Here are the keys to your new home, madam.'

'Thank you kindly, sir,' Helen said and curtsied.

'Of course you realise that we are a two-way deal now,' he told her. 'We both gotta pay half and half.'

She fixed him with cold green eyes, 'Right,' she said, 'you pay your half, and you pay my half. OK?'

'OK,' Angelo said grinning.

*   *   *

1952 was an important year in Angelo's life because he had got married. It was also an important year in the life of a skinny, 10-year-old living in Louisville, Kentucky, whose name was Cassius Marcellus Clay. His bike had been stolen; and he was steaming mad. The feisty boy was not going to stand for it. He went looking for a policeman and found one at the local gym. The cop, Joe Martin, seeing the kid was boiling over with youthful rage, tried to calm him down. 'Take it easy pal. We'll try and get it back. Do you have any idea who might have taken it?'

'No sir, but when I find him I'm gonna whoop his black ass.'

Joe gave the 89 pound Cassius the once over. 'Whoop him, huh? Say he's a lot bigger than you?'

'Make no difference. He dun stole my bike.'

Joe liked the spunky young kid, and asked him if he knew how to box, adding it might be a good idea to learn. 'Sorta even things up in case he's a big SOB.' Joe told him.

Cassius thought it made sense and joined the gym on the spot. Within weeks, he had his first bout and his first win. He never did find out what happened to his bike or the kid who stole it. He was a natural athlete with unusual strength in his legs. It didn't take long for the boxing fraternity in Louisville to hear about the talented youngster. Under the tutelage of Joe Martin, Cassius began collecting awards. He won six Kentucky Golden Gloves Championships, two National Golden Gloves Championships and two National Amateur Athletic Union (AAU) titles all before he was 18.

His loving parents, Odessa and Marcellus Snr, were naturally proud of their son, and listened patiently to the many times he told them that one day he would be the world champion, and everyone would know his name. They had tried to give him a strong work ethic, and to know the difference between good and evil – not an easy thing to teach a poor, black kid in Kentucky, a State with rampant racism. Nevertheless, Marcellus Snr and Odessa did a fine job and deserve much credit for training a son who was proud of his people, had a strong sense of justice, and had the sensibility and love of humanity to articulate the following thoughts: 'Service to others is the rent you pay for your room here on earth. Hating people because of their color is wrong. And it doesn't matter what color does the hating.'

The handsome teenager, like most boys his age, liked the girls, and they liked him, but boxing came first. Clay dedicated his life to his career. What gave him this fervent dedication? Where did he get this single-mindedness from? What was the cause of his burning drive to win? We can only guess. Did he need to show he was as good, if not better, than the next man? He competed as ferociously against black opponents as against white ones. This will to win was probably less about race and more about himself. Here was a man aware of his own being. He was at ease with what he was, a proud man, who never backed away from strong principles of right and wrong, good and evil. It's impossible to define the source of his magic or motivation. Clay said, 'A man who views the world at 50 the same way he did at 20 has wasted 30 years of his life.' He lived his life true to that belief with his mind always receptive to new ideas and thoughts.

However, the pressure of racism affected his life. When he returned in triumph to Louisville after winning the gold medal at the Olympics in Rome, Italy, in 1960, the town gave him a parade, but he wasn't allowed to forget he was a black. Even with the gold medal proudly displayed around his neck he was refused service at a local restaurant. How did Cassius react? He threw away his gold medal in disgust.

The Italians say, '*C'è sempre domani*' – there's always tomorrow. For young Mister Clay there would be many glorious ones, and for the just-married Angelo Dundee, there were wonderful tomorrows, too.

CHAPTER 8

The Cuban Connection

Two days after his wedding, Angelo left Miami Beach with his fighter, Alex Fimbres, for Havana, Cuba. It was the first time Angelo visited the beautiful but turbulent island of Cuba. The trip would lead Angelo to three great fighters who all became world champions: Luis Rodriguez, Jose Napoles and Sugar Ramos. During 1952, he trained them and used his expertise to improve their skills. He got them into shape and worked in their corner. It was also the year he first worked with the indestructible future champion, Carmen Basilio.

Two 16-year-olds, Ralph Dupas and Willie Pastrano, who were destined to become world champions were taken to Angelo by their manager, Whitey Esnault. Angelo welcomed them, fresh out of school in New Orleans, to Miami where they trained under his guidance at the Magic City Gym, in the southwest section of Miami. Angelo had seen them for the first time boxing in New Orleans, their hometown, and had been impressed. Although only schoolboys, they boxed like seasoned pros. Dupas had a list of wins that was amazing for a kid so young. He had beaten Bill Neri, a good, young fighter, who had worked with Angelo a few times. Ralph looked a good prospect, but it was the skinny Willie Pastrano who held a special fascination for Angelo. He was a sweet boxer with a sensational left jab, but it was his warm, easygoing personality that caught Angelo's attention. Angelo learned that Willie had only taken up boxing to lose weight. As a young kid he had been a Fatso and too embarrassed to take off his shirt, a feeling Angelo remembered well from his own childhood. It had been Willie's pal, Ralph, who had talked him into taking up boxing, and he began losing the weight. When Angelo first saw him fight, Willie was a lean teenager, who looked nothing like a fighter, but the boxer on the receiving end of his left jab soon found out that he was.

Angelo worked with the two boys in the Miami gym. They got into great condition. Their manager, Whitey Esneault, wanted Angelo to arrange them some two-minute-round bouts. In New Orleans, Whitey could only get six-round fights of three minutes per round duration, but Florida had different rules.

Willie had six fights through July and August and won them all. Ralph did nearly as well. Out of five fights he only lost one. Angelo grew to like the two boys, and missed them when they decided they needed to return home to New Orleans. They were just kids really and missed their families. Helen, too, had taken to the boys. They seemed to have brought out her maternal instincts. After the boys had gone, Angelo got a call from Whitey Esneault in New Orleans. He wanted to know if Angelo would be interested in becoming co-manager for the boys. Angelo agreed immediately and Whitey said he would send a contract. That night, Angelo took Helen out to celebrate. They went to a club on Miami Beach owned by Jake LaMotta, who Angelo had known from the Stillman's Gym days.

They had a great night and Jake picked up the tab. Helen was pleased about that, because she knew that Angelo would take her to the club again, so *he* could pick up the tab.

In Miami, the hurricane season is normally at its most dangerous in September, but Angelo was praying that this September would not be ruined by a killer storm, because on 22 September, Carmen Basilio was fighting on one of Chris's promotions and Angelo was working Carmen's corner. Angelo had met Carmen Basilio back in 1950 in Brooklyn, while he was working the corner for welterweight Mike Koballa, who was fighting Basilio. Koballa was a three-to-one underdog, but as so often happens in the fight game, the underdog won. Angelo, although pleased, hadn't expected that result. He had seen that Basilio had enormous talent and thought he would eventually get to the top. After the fight, Angelo went to Carmen's dressing room to pay his respects. The rugged fighter was sitting on the table, legs dangling over the side, his face puffed and bruised. He was partially dressed and was buttoning up his shirt as he answered questions from reporters from the local newspapers.

'Great fight, Carmen. I'm glad my guy won, but I'm sorry you lost. You got a lotta talent,' Angelo said when he got a chance.

One of Carmen's managers put his arm around Carmen and said, 'Thanks, Angelo. It was one of those things.' Carmen managed a smile, 'Yeah, thanks, Angelo. Koballa sure surprised me. I'll take him next time.'

One of the reporters put his two cents in. 'If I were you, Carmen, I'd forget it. You cut and bruise too easily. You ain't gonna make it. Why don't you get out of the game?' The comments made Angelo mad, and before Carmen's manager could answer, and before Carmen could decide whether to take offence or not, Angelo interfered. 'What the hell are you talking about? What are you, some kind of expert or somethin'? Carmen is a great fighter, and the only place he's goin' is up.'

That was the last time Angelo had seen Basilio, but now he was boxing in Miami, and Angelo was in *his* corner. Basilio, now with a big reputation, was fighting 'Baby' Williams, a very useful fighter. Before the bout, Angelo wrapped Carmen's hands, which was very flattering, because for the last three years, since he had broken a hand in a fight, Carmen preferred to wrap his own hands.

The fight was no walkover for Carmen. 'Baby' Williams gave him trouble in a tough fight during which he sustained a couple of nasty cuts over the eyes. The knowledge and techniques Angelo had learned during his years of apprenticeship in New York came in handy. He took care of the cuts expertly, without any fuss or undue trouble, but he never denied he was relieved when the bell sounded for the end of the fight, and Basilio took the decision. The bout had been over eight rounds, and Angelo certainly was glad it hadn't been 15.

Back home, having a nightcap with Helen, she asked if anything had been said by Basilio or his managers about using him again. Angelo didn't like telling her that nothing had been worked out. Other than thanking him for his work, nobody had said anything about any future plans. Angelo wasn't too upset as he knew he had done a good job. As it worked out, when John de John, Basilio's manager, paid him his wages for his night's work, it was more like a tip than wages.

If Angelo's spirits had been low because he'd been cold-shouldered by Basilio's management, the news he received from New York the following night should have lifted them. On 23 September, Rocky

Marciano won the world heavyweight championship by knocking out Jersey Joe Walcott in the 13th round. A few days later, Angelo called Charlie Goldman, the little man whose faith and guidance was so instrumental in Rocky's success. Charlie tried to give Angelo a blow–by–blow description of the fight, but Angelo had to cut him short – he was paying for the call and money was still hard to come by.

He was managing or co-managing a few fighters, but they were earning very little and often Angelo ended up foregoing his commission and earning nothing. He did make a few bucks from working as a corner man for whoever wanted him, but that was barely keeping his head above water. Angelo was still working seven days a week with Chris, doing a hundred different jobs, but he didn't get any wages for that. Being with Chris gave him a base from which to handle his fighters and pick up work as a corner man.

Helen never complained. They both knew he could earn more money if he went back to the navy yard in South Philly, but that was out of the question. They loved Miami and Angelo intended to stay in the fight game for good. Things were tough all over. Still, Angelo and Helen were happy. They had the same attitude his family had in South Philly as he was growing up. They didn't feel they were broke. They just didn't have any money.

CHAPTER 9

Frankie Carbo

When he agreed to a bout for his fighters, Angelo did his homework and checked out the opponents before he signed on the dotted line. He watched the other fighters and built up his own dossiers on them. He kept an eye on all the boxing results. He would telephone friends and ask them what newcomers were like and whether they could punch or take a punch. A good manager should know the fighters to steer clear of, but eventually, if a fighter is going to be a champion, he has to face every challenger. A manager can pick the opponents, study them, define their weaknesses, but that will not guarantee the result. That's in the lap of the gods.

There are often bad decisions in boxing, as in life. When you decide on a course of action, be it large or small, the consequences of that action are in the future and unknown. It's said that 'IF' is the biggest little word in the English language. 'If only I hadn't done that', 'If only I hadn't answered the telephone', 'If only I had caught a later flight.'

'If' was a word Angelo used a great deal after the Jimmy Beecham–Bobby Boyd bout in Washington, DC. It looked like a good fight on paper, between Jimmy, a middleweight who lived in Miami, and Bobby. It would be an action fight that would win friends. Beecham was tough. As a teenager he had gotten himself into some trouble with the law and had done a short stretch. He had straightened himself out, gone into boxing, and settled in Miami.

Angelo had had his doubts about Jimmy beating Bobby Boyd as Boyd was a shade too experienced. He didn't relish the thought of going all the way to Washington and losing, particularly as the weather forecasts warned of low temperatures, with a chance of snow. He did not even own a topcoat. All he knew was that Beecham had a reasonable chance of winning and that both he and Angelo needed the money so he decided to go. It turned out to be one of the worst decisions he ever made, and it had nothing to do with the result of the fight.

About two hours before the fight time, the sky over Washington darkened, and then, from the menacing greyness, the snow began to fall and fall. He had nothing against snow – it looked pretty, and it could be fun, especially at Christmas time. But the snow's timing was wrong. Angelo wanted to catch a plane to Miami after the fight and he was worried that flights out of Washington would be grounded. He wanted to go home. Helen would be waiting.

During the fight, when he was working the corner, Angelo didn't have anything on his mind except the fight and his fighter. His personal worries were shelved during the fights, and he concentrated purely on the job at hand. Not once during the Beecham–Boyd fight did he think about the weather.

The good news was that Jimmy Beecham earned a draw. It would have been better news if he had won, but he wouldn't complain about a crowd-pleasing draw. Jimmy had made a lot of friends and the crowd liked him. The bad news was that Angelo was snowed in and the flight to Miami was cancelled.

Jimmy and Angelo checked into a hotel. Jimmy was exhausted, and after ordering a sandwich and a glass of hot milk, he went to bed. Angelo went to eat at a restaurant popular with the boxing fraternity, Goldie Ahearn's. He sat in the shelter of the cab as he paid off the driver. He was wearing a suit meant for sunny Miami, not a snowstorm in Washington. He hurried into the welcoming warmth and cordiality of Goldie's. It hadn't yet filled up, or perhaps the fight crowd had gone straight home because of the weather. Angelo had eaten there a few times before when he had worked in Washington and Goldie Ahearn gave him a big welcome. None of his pals from the press was in the restaurant. Goldie showed him a nice table at the back and told Angelo he would join him for a drink later.

He hated eating alone. If he had known no one he knew would be there, he would have stayed in the hotel and eaten in his room. The place was getting busy. His spirit rose when a couple of the diners, as they passed his table, recognised him from the fights. They told him they thought Jimmy had won the fight. He didn't tell them he thought he was lucky to get a draw.

Angelo got the bill and asked the waiter to get him a cab. He began to thread his way through the now crowded tables towards the entrance when a voice halted his progress. 'Hi Angie. How ya doin'?' He turned to see who had spoken. Directly to his left were three men sitting at a table. The nearest to him was looking up, smiling expectantly at him. He couldn't place the guy.

'Hi. Nice seeing you.' Angelo said, with a false grin on this face. He was about to move on when one of the other guys said, 'Frankie thought Boyd won the fight, but I thought Beecham sneaked it.'

Angelo looked at the first guy again. He was still leaning back in his chair smiling at him. Angelo remembered the elevator ride in the hotel in New York. It was Frankie Carbo, the alleged racketeer, who had done a short stretch for fight-fixing.

'Sit down and have a drink,' Frankie said. His two companions moved their chairs and made room. Angelo couldn't think of a reason to refuse. He tried explaining that he was waiting for his taxi.

'No problem. Tell the doorman that Angelo Dundee is at my table.' One of Frankie's companions got up and went on the errand.

Angelo drank a glass of red wine and they talked boxing. He stayed five or ten minutes, then shook hands and he was out of there. Back in his hotel room, he fell asleep as soon as his head hit the pillow. Next morning, the snow had stopped and Jimmy and he flew back to Miami. The restaurant interlude went out of this mind, but it would come back to haunt him.

Two weeks later, Charlie Goldman called him from New York. The little man seemed upset. 'Angie, I got some bad news for you. There's a story goin' around that the New York State Athletic Commission ain't going to renew your licence.'

'What'd you mean? What's the story?' This sounded crazy. It had to be a mistake.

'The story is that Carbo has been under surveillance and they had a bug under his table at Goldie Ahearn's. The whole night's friggin' conversation was taped, including yours, during the meeting.'

'What friggin' meeting? I had a glass of wine with the guy. For heaven's sake. I've only met him twice in my whole life. If they don't renew my licence I can't work a fight in the State of New York. That means the Garden is out. If New York bans me, I'll be thought of as a crook! Charlie, what the hell is going on?'

'What can I tell you? The DA is investigating Carbo. This District Attorney ain't fooling around. He is fishing around every-thing. Bribes, syndicate infiltration, and the breaking of antitrust and monopoly laws. There is a lotta crap going down. Look, Angie, all I'm saying is you ain't looking too good. I thought I would give you the word.'

'Thanks, Charlie, I appreciate it. I'm clean. Hey, give my best to Rocky. Take care, pal.'

Angelo felt like somebody had hit him in the solar plexus. He felt sick. Sure, he knew guys who were in the rackets. He grew up with some in South Philly, but he'd kept his nose clean. For him, it was a 'hello-goodbye, pal' relationship. Now he was in a jam for not saying goodbye quickly enough. Angelo burned up the telephone lines speaking to friends in New York. They advised him not to apply for the renewal of his manager-second licence. He took the advice, but he also decided to go and see James Fuscass, lawyer to the Athletic Commission.

His meeting with Fuscass confirmed all that Charlie had told him. He was in bad shape, but at least there was no possibility of any legal action being taken against him. Fuscass told Angelo that the two police officers on the case, one a female, had said the taped conversation wasn't incriminating. They felt that Angelo was guilty by association. Fuscass felt Dundee had been unlucky to have been dragged into the case. Angelo thought he had been damn unlucky. One nagging thought remained in Angelo's mind – if only it hadn't snowed that night.

Under the circumstances, Fuscass advised Angelo not to pursue the matter of licence renewal at that time. The State Commission would be informed of his unwitting involvement in the investigation, and Fuscass assured him that his licence would not be revoked. In the following year, by which time the Carbo investigation would be resolved, he should apply as usual for its renewal, and it would be granted.

Angelo thanked James warmly, and although he would not be able to ply his trade in the State of New York for one year, he felt relieved that the Commission would know that he was an innocent victim of circumstances. The following year he applied for his licence renewal and got it, but he sure wished that he had not taken the Boyd–Beecham fight in Washington. If only...

Angelo had learned a lot more of what went on behind the scenes in boxing. You would have had to have been deaf, dumb and blind not to have known that it was teeming with corruption. Ray Arcel, who had taught Angelo the rudiments of working a corner and instructed him on what was going on in the corridors of power. 'If you ever get a champion, Angelo, you'll have to play ball with Jim Norris of the IBC (International Boxing Club) and 'Mr Gray', (just one of the names given to Frankie Carbo, because of his grey hair. Carbo was also known as 'The Wolf' or 'The Uncle').

In 1953 Carbo and Norris had a vice-like grip on boxing. Norris and the IBC took over the Mike Jacobs empire in 1948 and, from 1949 to 1953, all the 13 heavyweight championship bouts were promoted under their auspices. Carbo had allegedly been involved in bribery, fight-fixing and strong arm tactics on those who didn't do things his way. He was often referred to as a major mob figure. Since 1933 he had controlled – 'managed' doesn't tell the full story – fighters, mainly in the middle-, welter- and lightweight division.

Norris and Carbo were an unlikely duo. James D. Norris had come from a wealthy Chicago family. His father owned Stadia and hockey teams in the Midwest. The young James D. inherited his father's business acumen. Perhaps because he came from the city that indulged Al Capone and Frank Nitti, Norris seemed to have a liking and respect for muscle. Maybe that's why he took to Carbo. There was no doubt that he liked Frankie. He even named his racehorse 'Mr Gray'. The IBC had exclusive contractual rights for Madison Square Garden and its television deals. They virtually controlled it. And you needed to be a brave man to go against Frankie Carbo. He owned fighters, or the managers of the fighters. So if you were in boxing, somewhere along the line you had to do business with them. That is, if you wanted to stay in the business.

Angelo was just a 'nobody'. Chris sheltered him and warned him to be nice to everyone and keep his mouth shut. Chris could handle himself. He was his own man and he was liked and respected throughout the fight game. It was fortunate that he had moved to Miami, keeping well out of any conflicts and power plays that were happening in New York, and to a lesser extent in Los Angeles. Ray Arcel was not as fortunate. Attempting to run a Saturday night fight promotion for television without coming to terms with Frankie, he ended up being attached with a lead pipe. Ray knew who was responsible, but nothing was ever proven, his television deal collapsed shortly after the incident.

During Angelo's early days in New York, he was in a position where he didn't know or care who the backers were – he was just glad to be working. He called everyone 'Mister', and went about doing his job. After his brush with the New York licensing committee, he always made certain that if and when he met someone with alleged crime connections, it would be a very quick 'hello-goodbye' relationship. He didn't even want to be in the same room.

CHAPTER 10

There's no such thing as an unimportant fight

Angelo arranged three fights for Willie Pastrano in Miami. He won them all. In fact, he went through 1954 without a defeat, an improvement on the previous year when he lost three out of ten bouts. Ralph Dupas, the young boy from New Orleans, had a better 1954 too, with the only setback being losing to Paddy Demarco in New Orleans, but he won all his other seven fights during the year.

Dupas was a quiet kid, maybe a little introverted. It was amazing how he could soak up all the attention and glamour from being a star in the ring, and yet be so quiet and unassuming away from it. He was a great little fighter. Ralph was fast. He went from lightweight to welterweight, fighting the best of both divisions until he eventually made his mark as a junior middleweight. Ralph had to wait a long time before he got his due recognition.

Another quiet young man, Clarence Hinnant, was a light-heavyweight and one of the fighters who helped Angelo build a reputation in Cuba as a manager-trainer. Clarence had three fights in Havana, winning all of them, but he never became a champion. He was a good fighter, who, like a lot of professional boxers, never made the headlines or the big money. Clarence was a first-class athlete and a credit to his sport, as was the quiet man from Syracuse, Carmen Basilio. Every time Angelo worked with Carmen as a corner man, he felt Basilio would some day make a champion. Carmen was fearless, completely dedicated and a better boxer than many people, even the experts, realised. Being in his corner was always a worrying experience, because Carmen cut easily. In early 1954, Angelo had to prove his worth as a corner man. It was the Basilio–Langlois fight in Syracuse. Norm Rothschild was the promoter. Angelo had met him before and he was the kind of guy who had time for people. He spoke to Angelo before the fight. 'Do you have the black bag with with you, Angie? You know, the one with all your medical magic. I think you might need it tonight. Langlois is going to give Basilio a tough time.' He was right.

Carmen's eye was badly lacerated. The skin of the eyelid was split, it looked really bad. Angelo used the styptic ointment, which his fighters had affectionately nicknamed 'the Dundee ointment'. He also applied thymol iodine and alum. Angelo pressed the solution of chloride 1-1000 into the wound and carefully pushed the loose skin upwards until it was immersed into the ointment. He secured it with a thick layer of vaseline. The repair would hold until he was struck again. In between each round, Angelo worked on the cut and kept his fingers crossed that Langlois would get discouraged and go for another target area, like Carmen's jaw which was like granite.

Basilio got through the bout and took the decision, but after the fight they had to take him to the hospital, where his wounds were attended to. There was no argument that Basilio cut easily, but not once during the years that Angelo worked with him was a fight stopped because of cuts. It had to happen, Angelo felt.

Angelo didn't know when or where, but he just believed that he would be involved in a world championship fight. 1954 was over, and he wondered how long it would be before he realised his dream. He analyzed his chances. He knew it was too early in the careers of Willie Pastrano and Ralph Dupas, although Ralph was stringing together a lot of wins. Unfortunately for Angelo's bank account, Basilio's fights were nearly all in New Orleans. Angelo didn't really care about receiving any percentage from those fights, but it was making it difficult for co-manager Whitey Esneault to turn down the attractive purses promoters were paying, and let Ralph take less money to fight out of town and build up his reputation nationwide. Would Jimmy Beecham be Angelo's first title shot? Probably not. He wasn't ready. The other young, talented fighters that Angelo was involved with were just not good enough. It would have to be a fighter that he didn't manage, one he only worked with.

One fighter stood head and shoulders above the rest. In early 1955, Joe Netro, a member of Basilio's management team called to tell him that Carmen Basilio was getting a shot against Tony DeMarco for the world welterweight title. The bout was scheduled for 10 June in Carmen's home town of Syracuse. Angelo arrived in Syracuse 10 days before the fight so that he could be on hand for the final stages of Carmen's training. Although nothing specific had been said and he was only paid to work the corner as a second, his duties had widened. Angelo guessed it began when he unconsciously started giving instructions and advice during a fight. John de John and Joe Netro, who was the tactician, were nearly always in the corner with Angelo, but they let him control it and they never curbed his natural enthusiasm to say what he thought was best for Carmen. The instructions he gave seemed to work, and Joe Netro obviously agreed with what Angelo said. More importantly, Basilio agreed with what he said.

Angelo liked and admired Carmen. He was as tough as any man could wish to be. Because he cut and bruised easily, his skill at boxing was often overlooked. He could slip punches and hook with both hands. By any standards, Basilio must rank with the greatest. Carmen had a mind of his own. He was a man who knew what he wanted and was capable of getting it. He was meticulous in his preparation. Angelo had never before or since known a fighter who was so self-contained. He would arrive at a fight with all that was required for a boxer – bandages, tapes, cotton gauze pads, towels, vaseline, iodine and even a pair of scissors. Many of the guys Angelo had worked with arrived at a venue armed only with confidence, and even that you couldn't guarantee. Angelo was flattered that Carmen and the others had enough faith in him to let him control his corner in a championship bout. This was one hell of a thrill for Angelo. Since his days in New York he had wanted to be involved in a world title shot and this was it. Sure, he was excited, but he knew that he could handle the job.

Basilio's opponent, the reigning world champion Tony DeMarco, had not been defeated since 1952 which shows how good he was. He had won the title from Johnny Saxton, who had in turn taken it from the legendary Kid Gavilan. It was a time of tough, talented fighters. To become a champion you had to beat awesome opposition. Both DeMarco and Basilio were only 5 feet 5 1/2 inches tall, and would come in weighing around 147 pounds. They were two lethal packets of dynamite.

Angelo soaked up the atmosphere. This was for the world title. He felt he had made it. Angelo looked around at the packed auditorium. It was a magnificent sight and the excitement charged through him, making his heart beat fast and electrifying every nerve in his body. The bell sounded for the beginning of the fight. From that moment on it became just another fight because to Angelo, there was no such thing as an unimportant bout. All his concentration was on his fighter and the fight in progress. The end came in the 12th round. Carmen, bloodied and cut, nevertheless proved too strong for DeMarco, who finally fell to one of Carmen's unique right–hand uppercuts. It was over. Carmen Basilio was the new welterweight champion of the world.

In those days, there was only one world champion at each weight division, unlike today when there are four or even five federations, each with its own world champion. In 1955, to be welterweight champion of the world really meant something.

Early the following year, Angelo received an invitation from the Chicago Sports Writers and Broadcasters Association to attend their annual award ceremony on 14 February. On the given date, wearing his first tuxedo and black bow tie, he watched the after-dinner proceedings with growing excitement. The supremely talented Sugar Ray Robinson had been voted Fighter of the Year. Chuck Speiser, a college graduate, whose prematurely receding hairline belied his youth, was Rookie of the Year. The Man of the Year award went to Julius Helfand, the New York Boxing Commissioner. The award for the Boxing Trainer of the Year went to a delighted Angelo Dundee.

After the ceremony, flushed with happiness and emotion, Angelo spoke with Dave Condon of the *Chicago Daily News*. Dave was flattering. 'Congratulations, Angie. You deserve an award after the way you took care of Basilio in the Langlois and DeMarco fights. You sure did a number on those cuts. I'd have taken odds that the ref would have stopped the Langlois fight. You did a great job.'

'Hey, thanks Dave. That's what I'm paid for.' As they stood talking, the Boxing Commissioner of New York stopped by. 'Congratulations, Angelo, well done.'

'Congratulations to you, sir. Things have sure changed for me since 1953 when I last had dealings with the New York Commission.' Angelo smiled and winked at him. He winked back; he knew he was referring to the Carbo episode.

'That's right, Angelo, now you're famous. Isn't that right, Dave?'

'Why sure – Dundee the famous trainer.' Helfand and Condon nodded affirmatively and their faces split into beaming smiles.

Angelo knew he hadn't been Basilio's first-string trainer but it was his work with Carmen Basilio that got him the spotlight. He also knew that these knowledgeable sports writers and broadcasters were aware of the work he had done in training with Willie Pastrano and Jimmy Beecham. He gratefully accepted their recognition, but he knew he was not famous and he couldn't have cared less if he was.

'Hey, guys, I'm not famous yet,' said Angelo.

'But you will be,' Dave Condon said confidently. Julius Helfand smiled in agreement.

He felt that his life was going into another phase. It was a strange feeling which was compounded by an event later that year. On 27 April Rocky Marciano retired as the undefeated heavyweight champion of the world. It was the end of an era in boxing. Angelo felt Rocky's retirement was an omen. It was the end of an era for him too.

CHAPTER 11

The Sweet Science

It took Angelo around 40 years to develop the right attributes to play a major force in the careers of two of the most charismatic and skilful fighters in the history of professional boxing.

Dundee's life experiences forged his character, one that would enable him to fit into the diverse and unpredictable lives of Ali and Leonard. By the time Angelo teamed up with first, Ali, and then Leonard, he had learned the skills of a corner man, developed the art of motivation, experienced both winning and losing, suffered personal humiliation when he lost his licence in New York, but he never lost his integrity. And, perhaps most importantly, he knew when to lead, and when to be a team player. He always observed the right balance between 'coach' and 'buddy', although he was proof that a teacher can also be a friend. Angelo did his multitude of jobs to the best of his abilities. He was mostly oblivious to what else was happening around him as he focused on the work at hand.

He was a realist, and often answered people who told him how terrific he was, by saying, 'Listen pal, when the bell sounded I got out of the ring. I didn't take a punch. The fighter does all the fighting. I've never even got a bruise.' I really do not believe Angelo had any grandiose ambitions.

After May 1954, when he and Helen were blessed with a son they called Jimmy Steven Dundee, he had a family to consider as well. Jimmy was followed a few years later by the arrival of little sister Terri. To be able to live in Miami with his wife, Helen, and his two children was all he wanted or needed. To do the work he loved and to pay his bills was all the reward he asked for. If someone had told him that a young, amateur boxer from Louisville, Kentucky, with the unlikely name of Cassius Clay, would turn his world on its head, and make him the most famous boxing trainer/corner man/manager (he was all three) in boxing history, Angelo's response would have probably have been, 'Are you nuts?'

* * *

In the spring of 1958, on a beautiful sunny day in Miami, Ernesto Coralles, Luis Rodriguez's manager, was waiting for Angelo at the Fifth Street Gym.

A couple of days earlier, Corralles had called and asked Angelo if he would like to look over the Cuban welterweight champion who had only recently arrived from Havana and was looking for bouts. Angelo had seen Rodriguez fight in Havana and knew how good he was, so he agreed that Ernesto should bring Luis to the gym for a sparring session and he would check him out.

After the introduction pleasantries were done, Chris Dundee and trainer Luis Sarria, Ernesto and Angelo, all smiles and eager with anticipation began to get down to the business in hand – watching Luis Rodriguez in the ring. Chris had arranged for a couple of sparring partners to work with Rodriguez. Luis went to the dressing room to change and Ernesto and Sarria, like proud parents, followed him.

This gave Chris and Angelo a moment together. 'If you do a deal with Corrales,' said Chris, 'I'll put the kid on a few promotions here in Miami. You gotta put him in at a give-away price to me. After all, Cuban fighters are gonna be a dime a dozen. That jerk Castro is ruining everything.'

Angelo watched Rodriguez work in the gym. He had seen him in real live action, so he knew what he had, but he looked good just sparring. Willie Pastrano arrived dressed immaculately like a film star. Everything stopped when he stripped down to boxing shorts and training vest, entered the ring, and began his impersonations of other fighters. He got his usual laughs and he created a fun atmosphere.

Coralles and Angelo sat on two hard, wooden chairs that were part of a row of spectator seats, and came to an agreement: they would co-manage Luis Rodriguez. That evening, Angelo stayed in the office after Chris had left. He wanted to think. So much had happened since the Basilio championship fight. He wanted to get his head straight. Where was he going? He was working and travelling like a man possessed. He had so many things to take care of. Angelo looked at the notepad on his desk. After deciphering his notes, he concluded it was a reminder to take home photographs of the wrestlers for the kids, Terri and Jimmy. He took them to Chris's weekly wrestling nights. Chris was finding out there was a big audience for professional wrestling promotions. He was a boxing man through and through but making money was making money. Enough said! The kids were crazy about it. At the top of the page was Joe Netro's office number. He had to call Joe – something about Basilio? Could be interesting.

Since the welterweight title fight in 1955, Angelo had been a regular member of the Basilio team. He occasionally missed out working his corner if he was needed by Willie, Ralph or any other fighter in whom he had a percentage, but that was rare. Carmen's explosive career was turning him into a boxing legend. Back in September 1957, Carmen beat Sugar Ray Robinson, who was already a legend, to take the middleweight championship. Carmen then relinquished his welterweight title, not wanting to go down to the lower weight, which was getting harder to do as he got older. To Angelo's mind, he was not as effective at the middleweight limit of 160 pounds.

In the return bout in 1958, Sugar Ray Robinson won back the middleweight title in Chicago on a split decision. Angelo wondered if there would be a third confrontation between these two great fighters. But, sadly, American boxing was going through a power struggle, and a third and deciding bout with Robinson was lost in the political shuffle between the rival factions. It might have been one hell of a fight.

Against Angelo's advice Carmen's managers had agreed to a bout against Gene Fullmer. The fight was tentatively set for August 1958. Angelo had already asked to work Basilio's corner, but he asked himself, was he spreading himself too thinly? He felt he was involved with too many fighters. He managed, co-managed or worked on a freelance basis and all the fighters expected him to work their corner. And they were right. That's what they wanted and needed, but with too many fighters it wasn't always possible. No doubt about that, he'd have to cut back.

Angelo leaned back in his chair and thought about putting his feet up on his desk, but it was too cluttered. His back was beginning to ache. He stretched his arms and focused on the here and now. He turned to a clean page in his notepad, and began writing out a list of confirmed bouts and the names of the boxers he thought might eventually hit the real big time. He understood that a bad fighter can come good, but he thought he was reasonably accurate in his evaluations. In his opinion, only four or five of those boxers were world champion material. He listed Pastrano, Dupas, and Luis Rodriguez. The other possibilities were two Cuban fighters who he had recently become involved with: Douglas Vaillant, a very young 135-pound fighter and Florintino Fernandez, a junior welterweight at 140 pounds. Both these boxers were still inexperienced and had only fought in Cuba, but Angelo thought they had potential. Cuco Conde, a fight manager from Havana who had met Angelo many times during his visits to Cuba had recently called and asked if he was interested in another Cuban fighter. Angelo always found it hard to say no, so he hedged and told them he would talk about it the next time he was in Havana – God willing and Castro permitting.

Angelo knew he was a reasonably successful manager, with some pretty good fighters. He was also a top-class second and trainer who was part of the Basilio team and that was something to be proud of. Yet he felt in his heart he was still just Chris's kid brother. It wasn't that he was unhappy. It was just that he knew he hadn't really established himself. There were so many goals he had yet to reach. 1959 was just beginning and Angelo couldn't forget the old adage, 'Time waits for no man.'

Angelo had one hell of a lot of commitments in 1959. He had to

'It may look like an office to you, but at night it turns into my bedroom.' Angelo Dundee talking about Chris Dundee's office in New York City, opposite Carnegie Hall, where Angelo used to live.

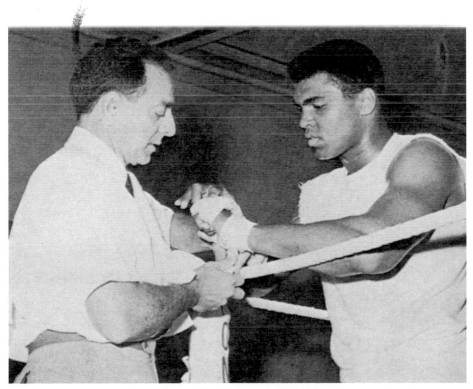

Angelo Dundee hand-wrapping Ali during a training session in a London gym.

Muhammad Ali avenging his earlier controversial win over Henry Cooper in 1963. Ali won this fight in London in 1966, in round six, when a deep gash in Cooper's eye left him no option but to concede.

'I'll beat him so bad he'll need a shoehorn to put his hat on' Muhammad Ali said before fighting Floyd Paterson. He went on to stop him in round twelve, on 22 November, 1965.

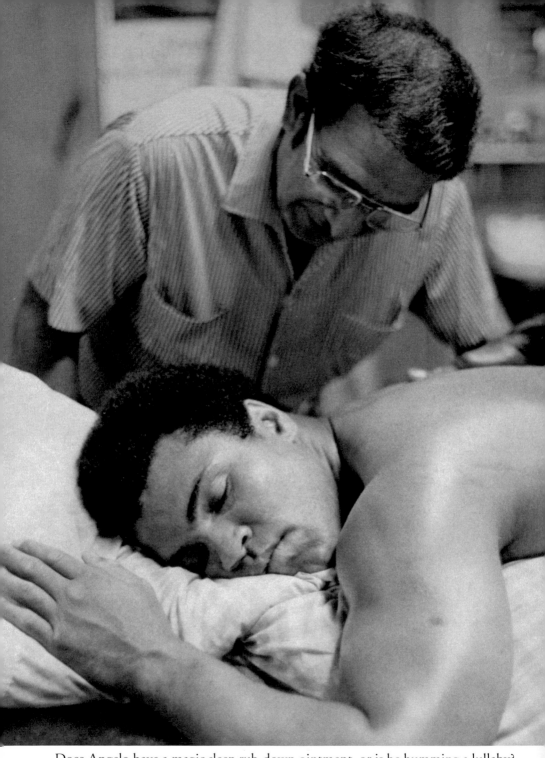

Does Angelo have a magic sleep rub-down ointment, or is he humming a lullaby? Ali gets a rub down and a nap while in training for the George Forman fight in Zaire in 1974.

Sugar Ray Leonard and Angelo Dundee at the weigh-in for Ray's 'pro' debut against Luis Vega on 5 February, 1977.

Sugar Ray Leonard and trainer, Janks Morton, jubliant over Ray winning his first 'pro' fight in the Civic Center, Baltimore, in February against Luis Vega in 1977.

Sugar Ray keeps his eyes on the ball. Training in Miami for his eight-round KO win in 1979 over Fernand Marcotte.

Dundee and Leonard after the fourth-round KO of the British Dave 'Boy' Green on March 31, 1980.

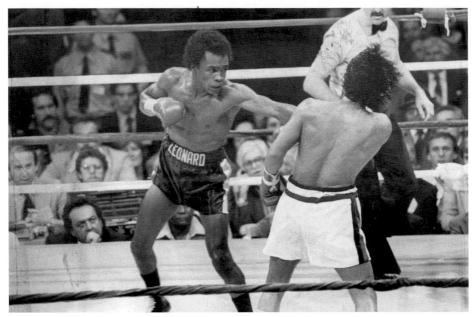

'No mas' (no more) Roberto Duran is claimed to have said at the end of their fight in New Orleans in November 1980, and Leonard became WBC Welterweight Champion.

To Betty : you remember when we were Both 39!! Angelo Dundee

The Axis of Greatness together in an informal moment in Miami. The photo is with permission from Betty Mitchell, long serving office manager for Angelo Dundee. Betty was like a favourite Aunt to Muhammad and Sugar Ray.

start arranging bouts for Rodriguez. He'd speak to Chris about that tomorrow, he thought. Dupas was fighting next month in Jamaica against their champion. He'd have to check his training and his weight. Willie was going to Louisville in July to fight Alonzo Johnson. He would need a warm-up fight. He had calls to make for Chris, and check on the publicity for Chris's wrestling promotion, and who knew what else his big brother would ask for. The list went on, but Angelo was tired and everything would keep until morning. He left the office, not forgetting to take the photographs of the wrestlers' home for the kids.

*   *   *

Without any introduction, July 1959 rolled in and Angelo and Willie Pastrano were once again on their way to Louisville, Kentucky. They left a day earlier than Angelo had originally intended. He thought an extra day away from the temptations of Miami, and an extra workout in the Louisville gym, would do Willie some good.

Back in 1956, Willie had initially made a big impact in Britain by out-pointing the six-foot-three Dick Richards, in October 1956. The British press loved Willie. Top sports writers such as Peter Wilson, Ken Jones, Reg Gutteridge and Desmond Hackett were real pros and appreciated Willie's boxing skills. At that time, Pastrano was probably Britain's favourite 'Yank'. It was a pity to watch that popularity slightly erode in 1957 with a loss to Brian London because of a severe cut eye and then his latest defeat in February 1959 to the excellent Welsh boxer, Joe Erskine. It put him in the role of an also-ran. Losing that last fight had taken away a lot of his confidence and his will to fight. Angelo had tried to arrange a few fights between March and June, but nothing came along that was acceptable. Maybe Willie would not make a champion. Many people thought so, and some managers would have taken their percentage and not worried about the fighter's future. Not Angelo. He had faith in Willie and had no intention of giving up on him.

When they got to the gym in Louisville, Willie seemed to cheer up. Bill King made a big fuss about them being there and reminded Willie that the last time he had come to Louisville there had been a horse race named in his honour, The Willie Pastrano Classic. Willie laughed and said, 'I'm entitled to have a horse race named after me – I'm a stud ain't I?' Willie went through the motions of training. Angelo watched him shadow box. This guy could be good, Angelo thought to himself.

'Excuse me, Mister Dundee. Remember me?' A voice interrupted Angelo's thoughts. Angelo looked up at the handsome brown face.

'Why sure. How are you doin?' For the moment, Angelo couldn't remember his first name. He knew his second name was Clay. He was the amateur he had met on his last trip in 1957. They stood by the ring together and watched Willie. The bell sounded, signalling the end of three minutes. Willie wiped the sweat from his eyes with a towel Angelo had thrown him.

'Hi, Mr Pastrano. You're looking good,' Clay said.

'Hi Cassius.' Willie had remembered the kid's name. 'How you doin? You still boxing?'

'Why sure. I'm gonna be in that Olympics next year. I'll be in that there Rome and I'll bring home a gold medal.'

Willie and Angelo smiled. 'I sure hope you do, Cassius,' Angelo said.

'Do you mind if I spar a round with Mr Pastrano?' Clay asked.

Willie answered before Angelo could. 'Sure, kid. Are you changed?' Cassius nodded and began to remove his tracksuit pants.

Angelo didn't normally like amateurs sparring with the pros. The inexperienced kids could sometimes be clumsy and accidentally hurt one of the other guys, or what was even worse, the amateur would try and make it a fight and win a reputation by decking a pro. If that happened, the professional could lose his temper and hurt the kid. Angelo didn't believe in gym wars. If you are a professional, when you fight you get paid for it. Everything else is training. Just one of the tips Angelo had picked up over the years that helped him become a great coach.

Clay climbed through the ropes. He towered at least three and a half inches over Willie. 'Take it easy, guys. Make it graceful,' Angelo shouted out to both of them from outside the ring.

It was three minutes of pure pleasure for Angelo. Not only for him. One by one the other guys in the gym stopped what they were doing and watched the two stylists box in the ring. Bill King, the promoter, placed an arm around Angelo's shoulder and said, 'Ain't this something? That's what I think they mean when they talk of the noble art of self-defence. Yeah, that's what I call, "The sweet science."'

The bell sounded and the two guys in the ring laughed at each other as they received a round of applause. Clay left the ring and sat down to watch Willie do another round of shadow boxing. Willie went into his impersonation act. After all, he had a captive audience. He shouted out the name of the fighter, then imitated his style – Kid Gavilan, Floyd Patterson, Gene Fullmer, Archie Moore. He closed his exhibition by shouting out the name Cassius Clay, and then giving an excellent impression of Cassius's individual style. Clay laughed louder than anyone.

The following day Cassius was again at the gym. Angelo talked with him, and came to the conclusion that he liked the guy, but he didn't encourage any more sparring sessions. Bill King, Willie and Angelo were having a light lunch after the training session. Tomorrow there would be no gym work, just the weigh-in and the fight. During coffee Bill King brought up the subject of Cassius Clay. 'What do you think of our local amateur champion, Angie?'

'Nice kid. Very talented. Made Willie work out for a change,' Angelo said winking at Willie.

'Made me look good,' Willie grinned. 'Nice boxer, gotta lot of good moves. Don't you think, Angie?'

'Oh sure, the kid's a very talented amateur. He should do very well at the Olympics. He's big, strong, and fast. But he bounces around too much, takes the steam out of his punches. Hell of a nice kid though.'

Bill King nodded in agreement, then said, 'If he can make the Olympic team, that's one thing. If he can take a gold medal from those Russians and other so-called amateurs, that's something else – then he's gotta be good.' They left it at that.

Willie lost against Alonzo Johnson on 24 July, and returned home feeling down. Angelo had just over a month before the Basilio–Fullmer fight for the NBA middleweight championship, and he wanted to get Willie into action quickly so that he would not lose his confidence. However, it looked like being a rotten summer: Basilio got stopped in the 14th round by Gene Fullmer, who retained his middleweight title. But four days later, on 30 August, 1959, in Knoxville, the sun shone on Willie, who KO'd Tom Davis in four rounds. Willie was still in the game, and if you are in the game there is always a chance of winning.

CHAPTER 12

A day that changed boxing history

It was September 1960 and the Olympics were over. Helen and Angelo had watched the competition on television. Naturally Angelo's main interest had been in the boxing, and when Cassius Marcellus Clay won the gold medal for the light-heavyweight division Angelo was overjoyed, like millions of other Americans, and kind of proud. Business activities pushed the event out of his mind until about a week later, when he read in one of the boxing magazines that Cassius Clay, the Olympic gold medal winner from Louisville, was turning professional under the direction of trainer Dick Saddler and boxer Archie Moore.

Angelo didn't quite understand the setup – Moore was still actively fighting and Dick, who Angelo knew was a good trainer, was training Moore. Maybe Dick and Archie had a piece of Cassius Clay, but more probably they were on salaries. They wouldn't want to wait for a pay day and who knew if Clay was going to make any real money. Angelo had things on his mind, like Tony Padron, a new fighter he was involved with. He was going against Cuco Conde's fighter, Jose Napoles.

Angelo was in the office trying to get things sorted into some order, when the phone went for the hundredth time – and it wasn't yet lunchtime. He was beginning to hate the sound of a ringing telephone. Chris was in the Convention arena with some television people from New York, creating more problems by giving them assurances that he could not keep – a typical day in the life of a fight promoter.

'Hello, this is Angelo Dundee.'

'Hi Angelo. This is Bill Faversham. I'm calling from Louisville.'

Faversham began a lengthy story about a group of Louisville businessmen who had got together to back Clay in his career as a professional boxer. Angelo said the appropriate things to keep the guy happy and give him a chance to breathe. The Louisville syndicate had made arrangements for Clay to train with Dick Saddler, who was currently working with Archie Moore, but Cassius wasn't hitting it off with Moore. Bill Faversham had brought up Angelo's name as a trainer. Angelo was well-known in Louisville. Willie Pastrono had broken the box office record for boxing attendance there. Clay liked the idea and so did the rest of the syndicate. Bill headed the syndicate, and he wanted to know if Angelo was interested and how he would handle the situation, so that he could report to the other members. Angelo was quick to make up his mind. He knew he wasn't going to turn this one down, but he didn't want to show his hand straight off. In the fight game, one must play hard to get.

'Well Bill, thanks for thinking of me. I gotta tell you, Dick Saddler is a friend of mine and a damn good trainer, so I don't wanna step on anybody's toes. From what I gathered, Cassius is in training for his first pro fight. I don't like to come in half-cocked.

Let things stay as they are until after the fight. Then we can talk but I'll say this, Bill, if I work with Cassius, as good as we all think he is, I'm gonna take it nice and slow, nice and easy. A lotta people who should know better forget that there is a big difference between amateurs and professionals.'

'It sounds good to me, Angelo,' replied Bill. 'Cassius fights on 29 October here in Louisville. I'll be in touch after the fight and we can talk terms. By the way, Bill King sends his regards. Take care.'

So that's the way it was left. At the time it was no big deal. Angelo had things on his mind and things to do. If Faversham got back to him, great. If not – what the hell.

As it got nearer to 29 October 1960, Angelo got more interested in the Clay fight. If Faversham did get back to him and give him a definite offer to train Clay, he wasn't 100 per cent sure he should take it. Angelo knew he was spreading himself too thin. His fighters were pretty active, and they needed him in their corners. Luis Rodriguez had won another couple of fights earlier in the year, in Los Angeles, and Ralph Dupas had made a couple of victorious trips to Australia, without Angelo. On top of all that, his Cuban pals were offering him co-managership deals with some good Cuban fighters.

Angelo faced a downer in Glasgow, Scotland, in September 1960, when Willie Pastrano lost a 10-round decision to Scottish light-heavyweight champion Chic Calderwood. When they had arrived in Glasgow, Angelo thought it would be a good promotional move if they went to a local church. As Willie hated flying, it seemed an appropriate gesture to go to church and give thanks for having arrived safely. The local press liked the idea and gave it a lot of coverage. A photograph of Willie with a Catholic priest got a lot of space. Little did Angelo know that there was a great deal of friction between Catholics and Protestants, and that the majority of fight fans and officials, not to mention Chic Calderwood, were Protestant. Though Angelo wouldn't come right out and say so, he couldn't stop a sneaking suspicion that Willie being a Catholic had any bearing on the decision. Willie and Angelo have often laughed about going to Glasgow. They didn't think of their Scottish trip as a real downer, more of a humorous but unfortunate experience.

Angelo was keen to see the Clay fight. He rang Bill King and let him talk him into coming up to Louisville. Bill was one of the syndicate backing Cassius. He was excited about the fight, and seemed pleased that Angelo was going to be involved too.

'Nothing's fixed yet, Bill,' Angelo told him.

'Oh, we'll get together. The kid likes you. Hey, do you remember how he carried Luis Rodrlguez's bag at the Atkins' fight? That Clay is something else.'

Bill was talking about the Rodriguez–Atkins fight that had taken place in Louisville in June. Clay had been at the gym, as usual, and was on cloud nine for making the Olympic team. There was no doubt in his mind that he was going to bring home a gold medal, then turn pro and become champion of the world. Luis Rodriguez loved him, and although Luis's English wasn't too hot, he and Cassius spent the morning in the gym joking around with each other – and working too. That night Cassius was in the entrance hall when Angelo and Luis arrived for the bout.

'I'll carry your bag, Mr Cuban Champion,' Cassius said, taking the bag from Luis.

'That's nice, Mr Gold Medal,' Luis answered.

'Save me buyin' a ticket,' laughed Cassius as he strolled into the hall.

That was then. Luis Rodriguez had been the attraction on that night back in June but now everyone would be watching the new Olympic light-heavyweight champion, Cassius Clay.

On the night of 29 October 1960, in Louisville, Kentucky, the time for clowning was over. It was time to see what Clay could produce in the ring. Everyone wanted to see the local hero in action. It was only a six-round contest, but after only ever fighting three rounds in his amateur career, it was an enormous step up. Angelo didn't know anything about Cassius's opponent, a kid by the name of Tunney Hunsaker, who is only famous today because he was Clay's first professional opponent.

The fight went six rounds. No one could deny Clay's natural ability, but his style gave a lot of hardened fight men the jitters. It was too unorthodox. They didn't want their fighters trying to copy it. Clay had too many bad moves. Angelo listened to the negative comments, which proved to be the sort of remarks he would be hearing for quite a while. 'He's off balance when he punches.' 'He drops his guard, he'll get nailed.' 'If I wanna dancer, I'll go to Roseland.' 'He's got no punch.' 'That dancing might be OK for the amateurs, but no way can he get away with it over six rounds.'

Angelo listened. There were many truths in the opinions, but the so-called judges were trying to compare Clay with other fighters. They were thinking how to change his style. Angelo never went that route. To him, each and every fighter was different. He never tried to change them, just improve on their individual skills and get rid of bad habits. And a bad habit was one that didn't work.

Bill Faversham called the next day. The syndicate wanted Angelo to take over as trainer, starting immediately. Angelo suggested they wait until after Christmas. That was turned down. Cassius wanted to start work right away. Before Angelo could ask what kind of deal they were offering, Bill said, 'We'll pay you $125 per week every training week and for the week of the fight, or you can have a piece of the action. Say 10 per cent off the top. What do you say?'

'Well, Bill, we've got a deal one way or another. Send the kid down here to Miami and we'll start work. As for the financial arrangement, I'll let you know which deal I want in a couple of days. OK?'

CHAPTER 13

The magic of Miami

A week or so after his first professional fight, Cassius moved down to Miami. He was met at the station by Angelo who took him to a one-room apartment, chosen by Cassius, in the cheapest part of town. He didn't have to stay in a joint like that as there were expenses to cover his accommodation, but Cassius had a pal sharing his room and he really didn't mind where he stayed. He was in Miami to train, to fight, to win and to become a champion. Where he slept was incidental as long as it didn't interfere with his objectives.

After a few weeks, Angelo asked him about the neighbourhood. Was it too rough? 'No problem,' Cassius answered. He had made friends, the people were just fine. Angelo realised there was a lot to learn about this young man. Each morning when Angelo arrived at the gym he was always there, ready to go. When the training session was over Cassius was the last to leave. There was always an extra minute on the speed-bag or the heavy-bag.

Willie Pastrano caught on fast. 'Is this guy for real?' Willie would joke, but there was respect and affection behind the remark. In fact, the atmosphere in the gym was terrific. Although at times Angelo thought he was working with the Keystone Cops, especially when Willie, Luis and Cassius were there together. There was a lot of ribbing about who would make world champion first. On the surface, you might have thought they were kidding, but Angelo knew better.

Angelo had to go to Havana early in December 1960, to work with Sugar Ramos, the featherweight fighter Cuco Conde wanted him to co-manage, and on 17 December Luis Rodriguez was going in against Emile Griffith in New York. Griffith was managed by Gil Clancy, an old friend of Angelo's from his New York days way back in 1949–1950. Gil had said that one day they would work together. He never said they would become friendly rivals but that's what they were. Angelo was looking forward to 17 December in New York, not only to see his old pal but also to watch Luis Rodriguez win – hopefully – in the Big Apple.

While Angelo was away, there was no need to worry if Clay was doing his training. Getting him to train was no problem – stopping him was another thing! Angelo wished he could engender the same dedication in Willie. Maybe hanging around Cassius would do him some good. Becoming a champion seemed to be eluding Willie, and Angelo was worried that disillusion would set in. Boxers are highly trained athletes, physically and mentally tuned to the utmost degree. They ply their trade alone and there is nowhere to hide. It is a marriage of top physical conditioning with unrelenting bravery. Boxers who carve a name for themselves are highly sensitive and complicated people. It is no wonder that boxing champions react in so many different ways to the pressures that fame and wealth bring. If you take the endurance of a tennis player, the courage of a race car driver, the sensibility of an actor, the continued discipline of a long distance runner, and mix those ingredients, you are on the way to knowing what it takes to be a professional boxer.

And what makes a great coach? Let's say, for the sake of argument, that a manager takes care of the business side of things and the coach/trainer – call him what you will – takes care of the sporting side and wellbeing of the sportsman or woman. The coach/trainer must be highly knowledgeable about the sport – in this case boxing – to earn the respect of the boxer. He must be sensitive to the fighter's emotional needs and know how to motivate, but be aware that each fighter is different. And it's a big advantage if the coach/trainer is also an expert cut man, someone who can spot the flaws of the opponent during a fight and instruct and motivate his own fighter. A boxing coach/trainer, although requiring skills unique to that particular sport, is a little like a movie director. The director doesn't do the acting but he can affect the outcome of the movie. A good director can make a bad script and mediocre actor look better, and a bad director can make a good script and good actor look ordinary, even downright bad. And it's strange, but good directors seem to attract good scripts and talented actors and have lots of hits. A good director cannot make a bad actor good but he can make him as good as possible when the cameras start to roll. And it's the same with the best coaches: they get their fighters to be the best they can by the time the bell sounds for the first round.

Though Cassius's controversial style hadn't changed, by the end of 1960 Angelo noticed the modifications he had made. He wasn't bouncing so much and was sitting down more on his punches. He knocked out Herb Siler in four rounds. Bill Faversham was delighted, and he thanked Angelo.

'Don't thank me,' Angelo said. 'I didn't knock out Siler, Cassius did.' Before Angelo left for North Carolina to join his family, he confirmed with Chris that Clay would fight again on 17 January 1961 in Miami.

Once he was surrounded by his family Angelo relaxed, but he couldn't help talking to Helen and to anyone else who would listen about the new fighter he was training. He must have bored everyone with his stories of how he had met Cassius and how things had worked out. One of Helen's relatives wanted to know if he was any good. He answered that with Clay's dedication and natural talent he couldn't miss. Angelo had Helen laughing when he told them about a phone conversation he'd had with Dick Saddler:

'So you're working with Clay? Good luck, Angie, you're gonna need it,' Sadler said.

'Yeah? What's the story? Didn't you get on with the kid?'

'Oh sure. He's some character. Cassius and I went by train to Texas. At every hick stop, deep in the heart of redneck country, he would stick his big black head out of the window and shout, "I'm the greatest". I thought we were gonna get lynched. He's some joker.'

Angelo laughed and said, 'He sure is, but I hear he didn't make a hit with Archie. What was the problem? One too many stars?'

Dick Saddler explained, 'Yeah, I guess you could say that. One day Archie gave Cassius a broom and told him to sweep up the room. Clay didn't like that. He said to Archie, "I didn't do that for my Ma," and handed back the broom to Archie. He can be a difficult kid. If you are gonna train that kid permanently, you deserve seven purple hearts.'

Helen liked that story. Many times in the future she would ask if he was earning his purple hearts.

Angelo hoped to return to Miami from his trip to Cuba feeling fit and relaxed so he could tear into 1961, but it didn't happen. He was playing football with the kids when he tried to demonstrate how the great running backs of the famous Rio football team of South Philly used to sprint and changed pace. He slipped, fell, and managed to break a couple of ribs. Helen and her sister, Frances, were watching and nearly collapsed laughing. When they saw Angelo was hurt, they were all concerned, but after helping him into the house they couldn't hide their smiles.

When Angelo returned to the office in Miami, Chris was on cloud nine. As usual he was on the phone. He waved for Angelo to sit down and shut up. Angelo lit up a full-size cigar, a bad habit he had picked up in Havana, and tried to ignore his aching chest as he attempted to make himself comfortable on his hard-backed chair. Chris eventually hung up and smiled broadly at Angelo. 'I got the Patterson–Johansson title fight. It's gonna be here in March. It's gotta be a sell-out. We're in for a busy time, Angie. We could make a lotta bread with this one.'

This was great news. Floyd Patterson, the former world heavyweight champion, was fighting Ingemar Johansson, the current world champion, for the third time with one victory each. Last time Floyd had lost his title to him and this coming fight would be the decider. It promised to be a great fight and would certainly pack the Miami Beach Convention Center.

Floyd Patterson intrigued Angelo. He had a fine record both as an amateur and as a professional, knocking out Archie Moore in five rounds back in 1956. He had a strange style, known as the 'peek-a-boo' style. He held his gloves high, hiding his face, and peeped out over his gloves. Angelo had watched him fight Joey Maxim a few years earlier, and he hadn't been too impressed. Joey beat him over eight rounds and never got a return. Angelo didn't blame Cus D'Amato, Floyd's manager, for not chasing after a re-match. Floyd was a puffed up light-heavyweight. As Chris told Angelo about the Patterson–Johansson fight, Angelo couldn't help but think that if the big, young Clay, 6 feet 2 1/2 inches tall and over 190 pounds was as good as he thought he was, he would have no trouble with the six-foot, 182-pound Patterson.

'How do you think Clay would do against Patterson?' Angelo asked Chris.

'You crazy or something? Patterson was a champion. Clay is just a kid. No contest.' Maybe Chris was right, then. In four years' time, Angelo was right.

1961 was a roller-coaster year of ups and downs. Cassius won his next two fights by knockouts. And in June, they went to Las Vegas, where Cassius out-pointed Duke Sabedong over ten rounds. That was an important step. The training was bearing fruit. Clay had proved that he had the stamina and conditioning to last 10 rounds. Angelo was becoming more impressed with his fighter after every bout.

Luis Rodriguez was having a patchy year, as was Ralph Dupas. As for Carmen Basilio, it was the moment of truth. He had another chance to regain the middleweight title. The middleweight division was in a state of confusion. In 1959 the National Boxing

Association had stripped Sugar Ray Robinson of his title for not defending it within the six-month limitation period. The NBA considered that the first fight in 1959 between Basilio and Fullmer, which Fullmer won had been a title fight, but the New York State Commission didn't agree. The two sides became polarised, and a chasm formed in boxing that resulted in the abundance of different federations we have today.

In 1961, Angelo had two fighters competing against two different opponents for the world middleweight championship! Carmen Basilio fought Paul Pender in April for the New York State Commission version of the title, and in August, Angelo had Florintino Fernandez, one of his Cuban imports, fighting Gene Fullmer for the NBA version. Unfortunately, Fernandez narrowly lost the 15-round bout on points, and missed his chance of becoming a champion, and Carmen, on a cool April night in Boston, fought his heart out unsuccessfully. The magnificent, lion-hearted battler retired from pro boxing. Carmen Basilio was a credit to the fight game, an honourable man, and Angelo's friend to the day he died.

Although Angelo had a great friendship and affection for his fighters, he never believed in letting his professional life cross over into his private life. When Angelo went home, he left one world and entered another. The camaraderie he had with his fighters was something he cherished, but it was never permitted to swamp his private or social activities. He believed in the old adage, 'familiarity breeds contempt'. He tried to make sure that it did not happen to him and his fighters. They had their lives to live outside boxing, and so did he. It seems to have worked out just fine. That doesn't mean to say they never communicated outside boxing. The Rodriguez family would occasionally come over to the house, and Luis's children would play with Angelo's kids, Jimmy and Terri, while the grown-ups would talk about boxing. And many times Willie Pastrano would visit with his wife Faye and their children – there were five eventually – but Willie was different, as he lived only a couple of blocks away and he was like family. Perhaps this hands-off attitude to fighters' private lives played a big part in Dundee's success. Of course, when a fighter came to him for personal advice or needed help over some financial problem, Dundee was always there for him. The money he loaned to his fighters and that was never paid back attests to that. A friend, yes, but doing his job as the coach/trainer always came first. Dundee and his fighters knew that was the way it had to be.

Young Cassius Clay was away from his folks, whom he adored. The Dundees thought he might enjoy a home-cooked meal, so they invited him over for dinner. Cassius called Helen 'Mrs Dundee' and was a big hit with her as he was with Terri and Jimmy. When the kids went to bed, exhausted after playing with Cassius, the grown-ups had a chance to talk. The men discovered they both had unfulfilled dreams. Angelo's were centered mainly on his wife and children. Cassius, unmarried at that time, wanted things for his family too. A beautiful house for his mom was top of his list. What he wanted for himself, more than any other material possession, was a brand new red Cadillac.

Angelo knew so many fighters who only wanted to take, and give back as little as possible. He would subsidise a boxer by giving him living expenses and personal spending money that was to be repaid from future earnings – if he ever made it and there was no guarantee of that. Some of them could spend money with a skill and dedication that it would be wonderful to see in their work ethic. Clay was different. He had this inborn sense of what was fair. He would eat at the famous Chef restaurant and keep the bills to show Angelo. That first year, Angelo didn't give him more than $5 for a meal. He would run to the Fifth Street Gym, and run back to the modest apartment room he shared with Allan Harmon, his Jamaican friend, who had boxing aspirations and who sometimes sparred with him and Willie. Cassius never once complained about his living conditions, or anything else. All he wanted to do was fight and improve, then fight again. It was a pleasure having him in the house, and Cassius enjoyed the evenings as much as Helen and Angelo did.

The morning after one such dinner, Helen was in the garden after Angelo had gone to the office, when she heard the neighbours talking loud enough to make certain that she could hear. They were saying the Dundees had a 'nigger' back for supper! The Dundees had actually let a black man enter their house and entertained him! Angelo was upset when Helen told him, but he had been through that scene in the army. He prayed that one day they would know better.

With Cassius fighting in Miami or Louisville, Angelo was home a little more than usual. He was home when Terri badly cut her big toe falling from her tricycle. Hearing her cries, Angelo rushed into the garden. He saw her ripped toe and blood spurting from the wound. He thought he was going to faint. As it was, he was sick and Helen had to drive Terri to the hospital, while Angelo was stretched out on the sofa. Once again the famous cut man had been KO'd by the sight of blood.

Life was good for the Dundees. The future looked promising.

The only recent blight on their lives had been the death of Angelo's father. Helen was supportive in this time of mourning, and her positive attitude helped Angelo face his sad loss.

Later in the year, they bought a red Desoto. Financially, they had over-extended themselves, but now they were a two-car family. Why not? Angelo was earning good money.

CHAPTER 14

Return to the Big Apple

'How many fights has he had so far, nine or ten? I'm gonna to leave the back a little longer. It's fashionable.' Mike Composto, the local barber, was cutting Angelo's hair and talking about Cassius Clay. Angelo thought he'd give him a free hand with the haircut and answer his question. 'I'll leave it to you, Mike. Cassius has had ten fights, ten wins.'

Mike talked as he continued to snip at Angelo's hair. 'Sonny Banks is a banger. He's tough opposition. Television coverage. Madison Square Garden. The kid is doing okay. Did you see the ball game on television? It stank. Moe Fleischer came in yesterday for a cut. He said that, as he didn't have a full head of hair, I should charge him half price. Can you believe that guy...'

Mike went on talking as only barbers can – not caring whether Angelo answered or not. Mike was Angelo's regular barber and a good pal. He was also a big fight fan. One of his remarks stuck in Angelo's mind. The bit about fighting Sonny Banks, the big banger the barber was talking about, in New York. Banks could bang, no doubt about it. He would be Cassius's toughest and hardest-punching opponent to date. Angelo believed Clay would win, naturally, otherwise Angelo wouldn't have taken the fight, but he knew it was no good trying to pre-guess results. Angelo sat in the chair as Mike snipped away, thinking about New York and this opportunity for Cassius to make a name for himself. Angelo knew the power of media exposure for a fight. He had discussed it many times with Cassius. If there had been a doubt in his mind about the necessity for publicity and promotion, it had been put to rest when they'd gone to Las Vegas the previous year, in June 1961, for the Duke Sabedong fight.

The boxing promotion for the Sabedong fight had been very badly attended. In fact, the hall was only a quarter full. The promoter, Red Greb, took his knocks philosophically. While they were eating, after the bouts, he voiced his opinion. 'You're a talent Cassius, and I ain't complaining. I took a gamble but I should have known better. No doubt about it, guys, being an amateur champ don't sell tickets, even if he's unbeaten as a pro. Nine or ten wins against nobodies don't mean nothing. You gotta have a big name bout top of the card. Too many other attractions around, not to mention television. If you want to pack them in, Cassius, you gotta build up your name.' Of course, Red was right. Although Cassius had done good business at his fights in Louisville, that didn't mean anything. He was a hometown boy making good. Las Vegas was a long way from Louisville. 'Stick around tomorrow night,' Red said. 'I'll show you what I'm talking about. We got wrestling on and Gorgeous George is headlining. This you gotta see.'

The place was packed, and when Gorgeous George, in his glittering robe, made his entrance into the ring, the crowd went crazy. Cassius was completely bowled over by the theatrical and outrageous George, and when they met in the dressing room after the bout, Cassius found it hard to believe that the astute and intelligent guy he was talking to was the same character he had watched in the ring. 'You see, Cassius, without my Gorgeous George image I would be just another wrestler. It's my gimmick. Without it this place would have been empty tonight. Right Red?' Red agreed. Cassius looked at Angelo. 'Of course, sir, you must have the talent to carry it off,' George continued, smiling, 'and a very thick skin. You sure get some abuse in this game. Not everyone loves me, but hey, everyone knows me.'

George could never have dreamed the effect his words were having, and that the polite, young black man sitting listening to him would also create a his own celebrity personal surrounding fights.

'Okay, Angie, we're all through. How'd you like it?' Mike placed a mirror behind his neck so that he could see the styling reflected in the large mirror in front of him.

'Looks fine, Mike.'

'Say, I was just thinking about Cassius Clay's fight in Vegas, last June. Remember? The Sabedong fight? Sure a good win for Clay.'

'Tell me, Mike, have you heard of Gorgeous George?' Angelo asked.

'Oh sure, the kooky wrestler. Sure.' When Angelo asked Mike to name another wrestler, he was stumped. He thought for a moment. 'Who knows wrestlers?'

'Exactly,' Angelo smiled enigmatically. He knew Gorgeous George had been right.

Angelo got back to the office, intending to take care of a few things. The last three months had been hectic. Work was piling up. At the end of 1961, Luis Rodriguez had met Curtis Cokes in a return bout and reversed the earlier decision. After that result, Angelo was hustling to get a title bout against Emile Griffith, but he was having problems. Teddy Brenner at Madison Square Garden, the matchmaker who would suggest or choose opponents, didn't like Rodriguez's style of fighting. It would have been laughable, except for the fact that the Garden controlled the Saturday night television fights, and that meant two things – big bucks and big exposure. Angelo felt sorry for Luis. He'd been unlucky. First, Benny Paret, when he'd been world welterweight champion between 1960–61, sidestepped him, choosing to give Emile Griffith a shot at the title in April 1961. Griffith won that fight and became champion, but lost the return fight six months later. The two great welterweights fought again for the third time in March 1962 and Griffith won back the title after giving Benny 'Kid' Paret a beating. Now they couldn't get Griffith for one reason or another. There was only one thing to do. Angelo decided to get Luis as many fights as he could manage. If he kept winning they would have to give him a shot at the title.

Angelo kept busy in the run-up to the Clay–Banks fight in February 1962. He started off in January with a 2,000-mile flight to Los Angeles, where he worked the corner for Sugar Ramos, who had knocked out Eddie Garcia in nine rounds. Angelo agreed with co-manager Cuco that Ramos had world championship potential. That win had been a good start to the year. Now it was February and time to go to New York for Cassius Clay's bout with big puncher Sonny Banks.

The New York press went for Cassius like a drowning man goes for a lifebelt. Angelo knew a lot of the press guys. He stayed in the background and watched Cassius turn on the charm. Love him or hate him, he had charisma, and those hard-boiled masters of their craft could spot it. Angelo knew there and then that if Cassius could deliver the goods in the ring, the press would turn him into boxing's biggest attraction. Cassius predicted he would stop Banks in round four. The sports writers loved it – a fighter who predicted the round in which he would win.

Cassius had fought outside Louisville and Miami only once before and that was at the empty Las Vegas venue. This fight was different. They were in big league country now. This was the Garden and Clay was going to fight as a five-to-one favourite, partly because of his record, but mainly because of the 'ballyhoo'. How could anyone that confident lose?

Being at the Garden was like returning home for Angelo but he was aware that the highly-charged atmosphere could put pressure on Cassius. He sensed the fighter's tension as round one began. Clay was too square, giving Banks a lot of target. Halfway through the round, Banks unleashed a fast left hook, catching Cassius on the jaw. He went down and stayed on the canvas for the count of two. Then he stood, taking the mandatory eight counts before being allowed to continue. For a couple of seconds, his eyes were glassy, but they cleared swiftly. Cassius had felt less pain than astonishment at being decked. There was no question of his courage or strength faltering. It was just his pride that had been hurt.

In between rounds Dundee told him to start moving laterally and stop standing so square – no fancy stuff, just take the guy out. In round two Cassius went immediately on to the offensive. He showed his speed of foot and the machine-gun rapidity of his blows. He caught Banks with a left hook, putting him down for a short count. Cassius went after him relentlessly. The same determined attack went on in round three, until Cassius sensed that he could stop Banks whenever he wanted. He let his plucky opponent finish the round, but in round four, as predicted, the fight was over, stopped by referee Ruby Goldstein, to save the helpless Sonny Banks any further punishment. The experts were impressed. Not only could the guy fight, but his prediction of when he would win was spot on.

Clay was on his way up. However, Willie Pastrano was nearly on the way out. Dundee had to make sure it didn't happen. He had always believed that Willie was a natural light heavyweight, but when he first began boxing, that division had no prestige and not many fighters. A guy could have gone broke boxing as a light-heavy, so they had gone the heavyweight route. But times had changed. Archie Moore was a light heavyweight and Archie was fighting and beating heavyweights too.

In 1961, the NBA took away Moore's title for not defending it within the six months regulatory limit. Winner Harold Johnson, with the recognition of both boxing factions, became undisputed light-heavyweight champion of the world. Where did that leave Willie? Angelo heard Archie Moore was looking to get back into action. If he could find a promoter who liked the Pastrano–Moore fight, and if Moore would accept Willie as an opponent, and if Willie could beat Moore, he would have to be in contention for a title shot with Johnson. That was a lot of 'ifs' and Angelo certainly knew how powerful that 'if' word was. Nevertheless Angelo got on the phone with a lot of fight people and subtly suggested Moore against Pastrano would be a great fight and big box office. Then he waited.

It wasn't long before Angelo got a call from Aileen Eaton, a highly successful promoter from Los Angeles. She had an idea to match Moore and Pastrano in Los Angeles in May. He congratulated her on coming up with such a great idea. Why hadn't he thought of it? Then they discussed money, negotiating until they were both satisfied.

Nobody gave Willie a chance. The story was going round that Moore had taken an easy fight on his comeback trail to a title shot. With his skills, Willie would never be an easy fight for anyone, although, admittedly, Archie was formidable. First winning the light heavyweight title in 1952 by beating Joey Maxim, Archie Moore had knocked out the current champion, Harold Johnson, back in 1954. Archie had even gone nine rounds with Rocky Marciano for the heavyweight title. He had lost that fight, but had gone on to win his next eleven fights, eight by KO. Archie was unbeaten in all his fights since the NBA had withdrawn their recognition of his title. His last three fights had all been won by KO's. Formidable was definitely the right word for Archie.

Even before they arrived in Los Angeles on 26 May, the press had taken an interest. Archie Moore had won his last fight in Los Angeles by knocking out Alejandro Lavorante and the media expected a similar result against Pastrano. Angelo knew Willie was fit, but would his lack of ring time, nearly one year without a fight, affect his performance?

Throughout the fight, Archie Moore was looking for that one knockout punch, the one that would put a finish to Willie and the fight. Every time he threw a big punch, Willie wasn't there. Willie was dancing. If he had worn a top hat and tails he would have put Fred Astaire to shame. Nobody could accuse Willie of being a big puncher, but he sure could box. The fight could have gone either way. Angelo thought Willie had sneaked it, but then he was biased. When the decision came in, it was a draw. For Willie and Angelo it was tantamount to a victory. Willie was back in the big leagues. He had to get a title shot, he just had to. Maybe not next week, or even next month, but it had to come.

The euphoria of the fight had died away and Angelo was back in Miami, scheming and hustling for his fighters. He was handling and working with a lot of boxers. Coping with all their individual personalities was like being a juggler. The difference was, if a juggler drops a club or a ball, it's just an accident. The guy just made a mistake. If Angelo goofed, he could ruin a young man's career and break his heart. He worked like crazy because he wanted success for these guys, nearly as much as they wanted it for themselves. Sitting on his butt wouldn't earn any of them a living.

All his fighters were different. The only thing they had in common was that they were all professionals. All had talent, but only one had that extra, indefinable magic that is as rare as plutonium, and that was Cassius Clay. Not only that, Clay had absolute dedication.

Luis Rodriguez was dedicated but was he totally committed? It was hard to know for sure. Luis, so affable on the surface, was self-contained, a hard man to read. The last time Luis Rodriguez had fought Emile Griffith, was in New York in 1960. He had lost that fight, out-pointed in the 10-round contest, At least, that was the decision. Angelo thought Luis had won. Gil Clancy and Howard Abert, Griffith's co-managers, laughed good-naturedly at Angelo as he relived the fight round by round.

Three years later, on 21 March 1963, in Los Angeles, Luis Rodriguez was getting another shot at Emile Griffith, but this time it was for the welterweight championship of the world. After the weigh-in, which went smoothly, the fighters were resting, conserving their energy for the confrontation that would take place that evening. Clancy, Abert and Angelo were checking out the ring. It passed their scrutiny. They sat for a moment looking at the vast empty auditorium, imagining how different it would all look in a few hours' time.

'Did you bring your own referee?' Gil teased.

'I left that job to Aileen Eaton, She's the matchmaker. I told her, "I don't care where the referee comes from as long as he's Cuban".'

'You gotta watch this guy,' Gil said to Howard. 'Do you know the story about Angelo and Bill Bossio?' Howard shook his head. 'Well,' Gil continued, 'Bossio is getting a hammering in the first round, then he catches the other guy with a lucky punch. The guy goes down. He's groggy, but not hurt. When the ref reaches five, counting out the sucker, Angie jumps in the ring and puts the dressing gown around Bossio's shoulders, as if the fight is over. The ref sees this and falls for it. He starts speeding up his counting. Seven, eight, nine, ten, out. The guy is counted out before he could get up! That's my pal, Angie. He knows more tricks than a Broadway hooker.' Howard laughed.

'Laugh, why don't ya,' Angelo said seriously. 'When Luis hits Griffith with his new special punch, I won't need to work the dressing-gown shtick. Emile can kiss his title goodbye.'

'What new special punch?' Howard asked.

'Forget it, Howie. He's trying to do a number on us,' Gil Clancy said grinning. 'That's Angelo, always good for a laugh.'

It was a fun atmosphere, exciting too. The Los Angeles fight fans were a good-humoured bunch. Angelo couldn't help wondering if this was going to be the night, the one he'd been tasting for 15 years? Would he finally realise his ambition to have his own world champion! It could even be two world champions, both crowned on the same night, because Sugar Ramos was challenging the featherweight champion, Davey Moore. It was a mind-shattering thought. He'd take it one step at a time.

Before they left the dressing room Angelo thought he was more nervous than Luis, who always seemed relaxed before a fight. He managed to hide well what nerves he had. As a boxer, Luis was fast and moved out of danger more times than not. He was a brilliant defensive boxer. He had been stopped but he would never take a beating. At the end of his career, Luis had fought 121 bouts, had lost 13 and had been KO'd three times.

The Rodriguez–Griffith bout went the full 15 strength-sapping rounds. It was a gruelling, action-filled battle, with both boxers refusing to lose. It was close, very close. Everyone awaited the decision anxiously. Angelo had Rodriguez in front, but would it be another bad decision? Not this time. The decision went against Griffith. Luis Rodriguez had won and was the new welterweight champion of the world.

Angelo had only a short time to enjoy the moment of victory. His heart was pumping like crazy with emotion, but he had to take a hold of himself. He watched from the corner as the new champion left the ring to the roar of the crowd. He was so happy for the guy. Luis had done his job, now Angelo must finish his. He had to get ready to work the corner again – this time with Sugar Ramos, against Davy Moore for the featherweight champion of the world.

Led by co-manager Cuco Conde, Sugar entered the arena. Angelo had sensed Sugar's anxiety when he wrapped the boxer's hands earlier in the dressing room. It was a normal emotion for boxers to feel just before they made their entrance. Sometimes, the roar of the crowd would change the mood to one of excitement and resolve. Many fighters lost their nervousness once the bell sounded for the first round and the fight began. And there were times when a great fighter froze, maybe psyched out by the enormity of the occasion.

Sugar had warmed up. His body was covered with sweat, but he was still a little tense. Angelo wanted him looser. Sugar did some stretching exercises in the ring as the champion, Davey Moore, made his entrance. Moore, five foot two and a half inches tall, was approaching 30 and had held the title for four years. He had won his title in Los Angeles. Many wondered if he would lose it here, too. The referee gave the two protagonists their pre-fight instructions. They touched gloves, symbolically shaking hands. The fight was on.

Sugar was too tight in the early rounds, and the experienced Moore was building up a lead. The pressure was clearly affecting the 21-year-old Ramos. During the middle rounds of the 15-round contest, Sugar began to find his rhythm and give as good as he was getting, but Angelo still had Davey in front. Round nine ended. The stool was there waiting as Sugar reached his corner. Angelo held the waistband of the boxer's shorts away from the body with one hand, and lifted the abdomen with the other hand, aiding the breathing. It was a manoeuvre he had learned back in his New York days.

After wiping Sugar's face with the towel, he gave the fighter a pat on his back for good luck as the bell sounded for the start of round 10. There was a flurry of blows. Ramos threw a right hand to the champion's jaw. Davey Moore fell, his head striking the bottom strand of the rope as he went down. The referee started his count.

Moore couldn't make it. The fight was over. Ultimino 'Sugar' Ramos was the new featherweight champion of the world.

The crowd went wild. A worthy chief had fallen to a young macho warrior. The many Latinos in the arena were ecstatic. Dundee rushed across the ring and grabbed the new champion. At the same time Luis Rodriguez jumped into the ring with the same intention. Then, with Cuco Conde's help, they lifted Sugar onto Luis's shoulders and paraded him around the ring. When the tumultuous applause and screams of excitement had died down, the proud, sportsmanlike Davey Moore came over to Ramos's corner, and with a grin asked Dundee for a return fight. Angelo ruffled the little man's hair and told him, 'You've got it.'

Back in the champ's dressing room, Sugar, a bunch of sports writers, Luis Rodriguez, Cuco Conde and Angelo were in high spirits. Angelo wondered if it had really happened. Two world champions in one night. Unbelievable!

There was a knock at the door. With a smile on his face as wide as the San Francisco Bay, Angelo opened the door. One of the Los Angeles newspapermen stood there. 'Come in, pal,' Angelo said genially, taking his arm. The reporter shook his head and said gravely, 'Davey Moore just collapsed in his dressing room during an interview. They've taken him straight to the hospital.'

For two days, the former champion lay in a coma. His family and friends, and many of the boxing fraternity prayed for his recovery. Sadly, it was to no avail. Davey Moore died in the hospital without regaining consciousness. Doctors established that brain damage occurred when he struck his head on one of the ropes as he fell. It was a fatal accident. His death sparked a storm of protest against boxing. No one outside Davey's family could have been more distraught than Sugar Ramos and Angelo Dundee, but they didn't blame boxing.

It seems a strong bond develops between competitors in high-risk sports. The camaraderie and friendship that exists in boxing is something quite unique. Fierce rivals in the ring, men who can bad mouth each other before a fight, almost invariably become friends when the fight is over. Like soldiers, there is an unspoken respect for brave warriors who face mutual dangers, even if, at one time, they were enemies. In boxing, there are rules of contest. An honourable fighter is respected throughout the boxing fraternity. The solid friendship that existed between Luis Rodriguez and Willie Pastrano and Cassius Clay was based on mutual respect. For Sugar Ramos, the death of his opponent, Davey Moore, was the death of a comrade, and although they were essentially strangers, it was like losing a friend.

Willie Pastrano getting a title shot wasn't exactly a surprise to either Willie or Angelo. The draw with Archie Moore put him in the picture and on 1 June 1963, the 28-year-old Pastrano was going to fight Harold Johnson the light heavyweight champion for the title. There was a problem however: Pastrano had fought only three weeks prior to the title fight. Would he be too tired, if not so much physically, then in his own mind? Would he be wondering if he would have the energy, the strength to go the distance with the world champion? A loss of confidence was not what the proverbial doctor ordered. Dundee began to psych up the Italian-American boxer. Of course he could beat this guy. He would box rings around him. This was the chance he had been waiting for. Nobody was going to screw it up for him – nobody.

When they arrived in Las Vegas for the fight, Dundee sensed Willie was ready mentally and physically. Knowing he was a 5-1 underdog didn't faze him. Willie knew Johnson was a big banger. So? Johnson would find he was not easy to hit, and his speed and stinging left jab could be very, very discouraging, and frustrating to an adversary.

Dundee gave Pastrano a light tap on his rear as he went out to meet Harold Johnson. Before the champ could settle, Willie caught him with a couple of sharp jabs. Johnson, stung into action, threw a terrific left hook, but Willie wasn't there. That was how the fight went: round after round, Willie landed jabs with rapier speed and when the hard-hitting Johnson threw a punch, Pastrano wasn't there.

Harold Johnson was a good, experienced fighter and he kept after the elusive Pastrano even though his frustration was mounting and Willie was beginning to get to him with a flurry of punches and then get out before he could be hit.

The champ's tenacity paid off near the end of round 14 when he caught Pastrano with a great right-handed shot. Pastrano's legs wobbled, but he didn't go down. Determination was etched into his face and his brain was still alert. He grabbed Johnson in a clinch and held on for precious seconds until his head cleared and his legs steadied. The referee broke them. Then Willie surprised Johnson, Angelo too, by attacking savagely until the round ended. Willie slumped on the stool and Dundee could see he was exhausted and still a little groggy.

'C'mon baby,' urged Dundee. 'Three minutes more and you're light heavyweight champion of the world! C'mon, for Faye and the kids.' Angelo went on to name each of Willie's five children. Time

117

was nearly up. 'Three more minutes. You're gonna do it for them.'

From somewhere deep inside of himself, Willie found new strength and he finished the fight in style. The two protagonists stood side-by-side in the middle of the ring, separated by the referee as they waited nervously for the decision from the three judges. It came. Willie Pastrano was the winner and new light heavyweight champion of the world.

The joy of achievement kept Willie on cloud nine for months. This feeling was shared by Angelo, who felt he had done a good job. When, years later, Willie was asked what Angelo Dundee had done for his career, Willie answered that without Dundee he would have had no career: 'He never gave up on me, and he gave me the confidence to be a world champion.'

The old adage held true: 'What goes up, must come down.' Two years after winning the title, Pastrano lost it to Jose Torres. There was no thought of a return fight. Willie not only lost the championship but his will to fight again. In 1965, he finally quit boxing for good. Dundee didn't try to dissuade him. He knew the time had come to let go. However, he was concerned for Willie's future. Unfortunately, Willie had begun to hang out with a wild bunch who were no strangers to drugs. Could it have affected Willie's last fight? It is doubtful. The young Torres was just too good for the older Pastrano.

Sadly, Willie sank into an alcohol-fuelled existence, becoming a shell of his former self. The support from Dundee was of some help, but the will to turn his life around had to come from Willie himself. I am pleased to write that, in time, it happened. Willie started a new life in his old city of New Orleans, Louisiana, counselling youngsters on the evils of booze and drug use. When I asked him about his work he said, showing he still had his old sense of humour, 'The kids know that when I tell 'em drugs are bad, I really know what I'm talking about. I can even tell 'em if they've been paying too much for their shit.'

CHAPTER 15

Saved by the bell

1963 was a phenomenal year for Angelo Dundee. He became co-manager of four world champions – Ralph Dupas was the fourth to join that exclusive club. After competing for the lightweight title and losing, and competing for the welterweight title and losing, Ralph beat reigning world champion Danny Moyer to become the junior middleweight champion of the world.

The Dundee office phone rang off the hook with newspapermen looking for stories, but not about the champions. It was for anything on Cassius Clay. The sports writers knew that Clay was one of a kind. Could he be the one fighter that would galvanise the public to watch the current heavyweight champion defend his title. Not that the champion wasn't good. The problem was he was too good. Then champion Sonny Liston overwhelmed the heavyweight division. His skill, punching power and threatening demeanour intimidated his opponents. The young talented Clay, with his confidence and non-stop mouth might, just might, create interest in that fight. Of course, everyone believed that Clay couldn't hope to win it, but to see the flashy upstart get his comeuppance would make an interesting story anyway. No doubt about it, Clay was news, and that was just what the press thrived on.

It would have been a big payday for the Clay team, but Dundee nixed any idea of the fight. Cassius was only 21 and it was too soon for him to fight a monster like Liston. Not that Cassius thought so. He believed he could beat anyone out there. 'I am The Greatest.' Would he be intimidated by Liston or any other fighter? The thought's enough to make anyone laugh. Clay truly believed that champions have something special deep inside them – a desire, a vision, a hidden reserve of stamina and they have the skill and the will to win. But, most importantly, the will must be stronger than the skill.

With the Liston fight put on hold for the future, Clay was off to England to fight the British champion, Henry Cooper on 18 June 1963. Henry was loved by his British fans. He was blessed with a great left hook and the heart of a lion. Unfortunately, he cut and bled easily. Without the disadvantage, Henry would surely have been a major fighter, not only in Europe, but also in the United States. Though the flamboyant Clay was already a big name in England and often impersonated by their star comics, his loud-mouth bragging, which were treated as an amusing gimmick in America, were regarded as conceit and damn bad manners by the Brits. The fans hoped 'our 'Enery' would teach the Yank a good lesson.

Currently, only around 11 per cent of the American public owns a passport. That figure would have been considerably lower in 1963. Going from Louisville to Europe was a big deal. That kind of travel was for the rich and famous, not for poor, black, 21-year old men from Louisville, where most white owned restaurants refused to serve them. For Cassius, it was a little different. He had travelled to

Rome as a teenager with the USA boxing team, but this was different. He was going to London – where they spoke his language – on his own merit. He was now a man, celebrity and an independent person.

When Clay was in London to fight Cooper, he was not his normal self. He may have been surprised at the heart-warming welcome he received on his arrival. Of course, there was bigotry and prejudice in Britain. Clay was no fool and he knew that. But he also knew Britain hadn't lynched Negroes, nor excluded them from any university. Neither were there any restrictions on where they ate. Because of his awareness and interest in his race, he also knew that Britain had abolished its slave trade 50 or so years before the American Civil War. This was the America of Cassius's youth. It had changed, was still changing, he knew that – but his scars from intolerance were raw and would take a long time to heal.

The press and public ate up Clay's theatrics, even when he predicted he would stop Henry Cooper in round five. The English do not like a show off, but they thought Clay was fun and accepted his bragging until he went too far and called Cooper a 'bum'. The English were angry. Their affection for Clay zeroed, although I must tell you it returned in abundance in later years. In other words, they hoped he'd get a 'whupping'.

Wembley Arena was packed with noisy, excited fight fans. It had the atmosphere of a world title fight, which of course it wasn't. But the crowd knew that the winner would probably get a shot at the world title. Dundee believed Clay should wait regardless of the result. The hostility towards Clay was strangely good humoured, perhaps because they thought Cooper would win. He was a good fighter with a great left hook. True, he cut easily, but the British fans, wearing rose–coloured glasses, believed their 'Enery would triumph, probably by a knockout. As things transpired, they weren't as crazy as the boxing experts thought, and that included Angelo Dundee.

The first three rounds were by no means one-sided. In fact, Cooper, with the crowd urging him on, was looking good. The picture changed in round four. Cooper's left eye was badly cut and blood began pouring down his face like a waterfall, obscuring his vision. Clay, with his hands at his sides, stood in front of Cooper taunting him, trying to humiliate his blood-soaked combatant. There were only seconds remaining in the round. Would the referee stop the fight? Cooper's rage was palpable. As far as he was concerned the fight was definitely not over yet. Squinting at his tormentor through the flow of blood, Cooper led with a left jab. Clay eased away, instinctively preparing for a right cross to follow. Cooper fooled him. He threw a long left hook. His signature punch, known as Henry's Hammer. It caught Clay on the jaw. His eyes glazed. His legs buckled. Clay was on the canvas. The referee began the count. When he reached four, the bell sounded for the end of the round. The well-worn adage, 'saved by the bell', was never more apt.

Many people, including Dundee, disagree with my assessment. They point out that somehow Clay dragged himself to his feet, proving he would have got up whether the bell had sounded or not. Clay was aimlessly staggering around the ring. If Dundee hadn't run along outside the ring and managed to grab Clay's arm so he could manouevre him back to his corner, the referee may have stopped the fight. Most agree that if the round had gone on for another half a minute, Henry Cooper would have stopped Cassius Clay. The round ended and Clay was slumped on his stool, like a patient recovering from an anaesthetic. Angelo Dundee quickly, without panic, began his work. He gave the distressed fighter a whiff of smelling salts, doused his head with cold water, and slapped his face until the eyes cleared. Then Dundee got close to his face and shouted at him. What he shouted we'll never know and Angelo can't remember. He only knows he shouted, or, more accurately, yelled.

We now come to one of boxing's most controversial stories which hangs on the question: Did Angelo Dundee split Clay's glove to give the fighter more time to recover from Henry Cooper's famous left hook? Here is Angelo's side of the story:

'As I was loosening and stretching his arms, getting the blood flowing through the tightened muscles, I saw a small split along the seam of the boxing glove. I had noticed the tear after the first round. It wasn't big, but it was there, and it shouldn't have been. I stuck my finger in the split, helping it along – now it was a bigger split. I yelled for Tommy Little, the referee, to examine the glove. I yelled at Teddy Waltham, the Secretary of the British Boxing Board of Control. I yelled at Jack Onslow Fane, the President of the BBBofC. I yelled at everybody. I wanted a new pair of gloves, but hopefully not too quickly. I wanted time for Cassius to get himself together more! I don't know how many minutes I gained, and I admit it was gamesmanship, but it was advantageous to both fighters.'

Considering the severity of the cut Henry had received, time was of the essence for him, too. His cut man had been gifted with extra time to work on the bloody eye. Who benefited the most? As no spare set of gloves was available, Clay continued to wear the original pair. And, as Cooper continued to bleed, Tommy Little stopped the fight one minute into the fifth round. Clay had won a fight he would always remember.

Although the Cooper–Clay fight does not have the glamour or fame of some of the later Ali fights, it was an invaluable experience for Clay, and it had long-term significance. Nowadays, it is mandatory to have spare sets of boxing gloves at ringside (they are kept underneath the ring). Cassius Clay graciously apologised to Henry Cooper, and although Clay stopped him in six rounds in a return bout, the two fighters became, and have remained, good friends until this day. Angelo's wizardry in the corner exemplified how important a great corner man can be.

One other incident that Dundee handled without fuss, and which certainly kept Clay's popularity from being ruined in England, was when Cassius had entered the ring wearing a regal looking robe and a royal crown. It had been slightly amusing before the bout started, but after the controversial fight, if Clay had left the ring wearing the robe and crown, all hell may have broken lose. Angelo normally suggested things to Clay. This one time he told him, 'Don't wear the robe or crown.' Wisely, Cassius agreed.

Bill Faversham, head of the syndicate representing Clay, confirmed a forthcoming Clay–Liston fight for the world heavyweight championship. Dundee wasn't too pleased about it. He would have liked to have waited until Clay was a little older, but he understood the attraction of a big payday for the syndicate. Angelo didn't know Clay's financial arrangement with the syndicate. He believed it would be fair, and never tried to find out.

He realised he had made a mistake in his own financial arrangement with the syndicate. When he first started with Cassius, he was offered a salary or a percentage. On Chris's advice, he took the certainty of wages, but now, with a world title on the table, a percentage deal would have gotten him a lot more money. This really didn't bother Angelo. He struck the deal and besides, he loved working with the brash, talented fighter from Louisville. Money was just a necessary commodity, that's all. Cassius understood this, and would remember. Right now, his world was moving quickly. There were too many thoughts in his head, but he focused on the prime target – beating Sonny Liston and Cassius Clay becoming champion of the world.

CHAPTER 16

Clay to Ali

The Clay–Liston fight was scheduled for 25 February 1964, at the Convention Center on Miami Beach. Obviously, Angelo's relationship with Bill Faversham, the head of the syndicate, gave his brother, Chris, an inside track in negotiating a deal for the title fight. For Chris and Angelo, they were at home and Cassius was in his virtual second home. The big night was only weeks away and they should have been feeling happy with the anticipation of a momentous victory, but there was a problem. For Chris, it was a 'biggie' – one that hit him right in the pocketbook.

The public had gone cold on Cassius. Unflattering stories, inaccurate and slanted, had started to appear in the press. One story reported he had charged the fans for his autograph. That was true. What wasn't reported was that all the money received went to a black hospital in Miami. The underlying cause for the media's hostility was Cassius's growing involvement with the Black Muslim movement. It seemed he had been attending meetings for a considerable time. At the local mosque in Miami, Clay was introduced to Malcolm X, who sparked Clay's interest in the Nation of Islam.

The Black Muslims were aggressive and termed white Americans as 'white devils'. They often preached physical resistance to any police actions they termed as racist, and were vehemently against interracial marriage. The American Olympic hero was tarnishing his image. Unfortunately, it showed at the box office. Fight fans were not booking to see an unpopular champion they considered unbeatable, fight an ungrateful, anti-Christian, overrated, Muslim-loving fighter from Louisville, Kentucky. It looked as though it would be a financial disaster but when fight night arrived, business had picked up a little. Chris Dundee wasn't crying. In fact, the fight was a financial success and proved to be unexpected to say the least.

Liston's fearsome reputation was built mainly on his two first-round knockouts of former champion, Floyd Patterson. Patterson may have been psyched out by the bigger and awesome presence of Liston. Even top class fighters can freeze for a second or two, time enough to get nailed. It happened to Patterson, and this might be what it happened to Liston. Perhaps, for the first time in his career, his opponent (Clay) wasn't scared. Worse, he didn't respect him. Sonny must have been uneasy. Tension can numb the reflexes. Sometimes, fear, which in no way means cowardice, can immobilise you. In boxing, you do not always have the luxury of having time to recover. Fighting without confidence is like swimming against the tide. It's tough.

The first round was toreador Clay against the bull, Liston. The second and third rounds were tense but uneventful. Clay landed a couple of blows of no power, but Liston, try as he may, couldn't land anything of consequence on the elusive Clay. The bell sounded for the end of round four. Clay looked agitated as he sat upright on the stool. He was blinking and grimacing with discomfort. Angelo recounts the incident:

'Cassius screamed at me that he couldn't see. His eyes were burning. I sniffed and tasted the towel I had just used to wipe around his eyes. There was something wrong. I tasted a strange substance. Perhaps something from Liston's gloves or hair. Perhaps a jet of perspiration had caused the stinging, blinding sensation in Cassius's eyes – I didn't know. All I knew was Cassius was hollering he couldn't see.'

His past experience as a corner man took over and Angelo began washing out Clay's eyes with a cold water sponge. It has been written about many times that Cassius yelled at Angelo to cut off his gloves because he was going home.

'No way.' Angelo wasn't debating. 'Get in there and fight. If you can't see, keep away from him until your eyes clear. This is the big one. Nobody walks away from the heavyweight championship.'

The bell sounded for round five. The ref had noticed that something wasn't right in their corner and started to walk towards them. To stop Ali from saying anything Dundee put Clay's mouthguard back in and shoved him forward, saying, 'Get in there and fight. This is what we came here for, baby.'

Cassius followed Angelo's advice. He danced away from Liston, magically avoiding his punches until the round blessedly ended. Clay had escaped the clutches of the champion, and his eyes had cleared. The next round, Clay, full of confidence, began to take the fight to Liston, opening up a cut under his left eye. When the round came to a close, despair and frustration were etched in Liston's face.

Clay sat easily in his corner as Angelo did his maintenance work. What instructions, or as Angelo puts it, suggestions, did he give

Cassius? At that stage of the fight, Cassius knew exactly what to do. As the bell sounded for round seven, Clay was up, ready and eager, but there was no movement from Liston's corner. Sonny Liston's large, muscular frame was slumped on his stool. He made no attempt to get up. The referee, like everyone else, was puzzled. Liston's corner men conferred briefly. Liston stayed on his stool. Slowly, everyone realised he was doing what Angelo Dundee had refused to let Clay do – opt out of the heavyweight championship. He let Cassius Clay, a seven to one underdog, become the new heavyweight champion of the world.

The surprising finish to the Clay–Liston fight created havoc both in the press and with the public. 'It was Fixed', 'Liston's Mob Connections', 'Liston threw it for the Big Payday Return Fight' screamed the headlines. It was an understandable reaction. Boxing had a dirty past with a crime-riddled history. There were stories going around about Liston's association with gangsters, lots of stories, lots of rumours, but not much evidence, if any, to back them up. Cassius was not included in any of the 'fight fixing' allegations. The fact that Dundee literally kept Clay in the bout, even after he had the foreign substance in his eyes, showed that Clay's corner had come to win. If any mobsters had taken the seven-to-one odds on Clay winning, why would they have tried to fix his eyes? Of course, it's all pure speculation. From my long friendship with Angelo Dundee, and my personal knowledge of Muhammad Ali, the mere idea that they would ever be involved in fixing a fight is not only ridiculous, to me, it's impossible.

Anyway, the media had an even juicier story to work on. Cassius Clay was no more. The heavyweight champion of the world, sometimes called the 'Louisville Lip' or simply 'The Greatest', was known from 5 March 1964 by the name of Cassius X. It was the name given to him by Malcolm X of the Black Muslims, the X reflecting the unknown name that was taken from his family by the slave owners many years ago. That evening Nation of Islam leader Elijah Muhammad announced on the radio that Cassius X would be graced with the Muslim name Muhammad Ali, meaning 'worthy of praise', 'fourth rightly-guided caliph'.

The media's reaction was immediate and hostile. The public treated the news with shock, ridicule and scorn. In the main, there was a 'who gives a damn?' attitude. Racism was still alive and well in America. Many asked, 'Who the hell was the Nation of Islam? Black Muslims? Ain't they Arabs, or sumthin'? They're all just troublemakers. Cassius X! He's just copying that Malcolm X guy. Just damn black commies, that's all.'

There wasn't a lot of understanding or sympathy for Cassius's action. The situation became more confusing when Herbert Muhammad, the eldest son Elijah Muhammad, confirmed the Muslim name Muhammad Ali. It was his new name and the only one he would answer to. Many people had a problem with this. Sugar Ray Robinson, Muhammad's hero, was one of them and it soured their relationship. Other sports figures, too, couldn't, or didn't want to accept the new name. But Muhammad was very serious about it. That was his name and that was the name you called him. If you didn't, Muhammad would remember the insult. The boxer, Ernie Terrell, refused, and when he and Ali met in the ring in 1967, Ali beat Terrell severely, taunting him throughout the fight with, 'What's my name?' Ali had taunted Floyd Patterson in a similar fashion. On 22 November 1965, Muhammad Ali had out-boxed, to a point of humiliation, the brave and clearly over matched Floyd

Patterson. Finally, and perhaps mercifully, Ali knocked Floyd out in the 12th round. Patterson was an outspoken critic of Ali and the movement, which actively discouraged interracial or interfaith marriages. But this was true of other religions such as Orthodox Judaism and Catholicism. Marrying outside one's faith or racial classification, was, and still is, unwelcome, even forbidden in many societies and cultures. If Ali had, or has, that particular strain of prejudice, it does not alter the fact that all through his life he constantly demanded equality for his race. As Ali himself once said, 'Small streams, large oceans, lakes, and ponds all have different names, but they all contain water. And religions, with different names, all contain truths.' Regardless of what Ali thought of Patterson's personal attacks on the Black Muslims and his new name, he had respect for Patterson's contribution to the sport of boxing.

The Clay metamorphosis into Ali took place in front of a backdrop of America's war in Vietnam. The attitude in the country was one of a slow fermentation of anti-government feelings. There was a dichotomy between the supporters of 'antiwar', and the 'stay the course for victory'. Still, life went on, and Muhammad Ali went on training and fighting.

At this point, Angelo could have quit. After all, how attractive could it have been, for a white guy in the sixties, to be associated with the unpopular Black Muslims? Conversely, as far as the Nation of Islam was concerned, who the hell needed a 'honkie' in their group of 'brothers'. Angelo didn't see colour. He saw the person. Since his army days, he had despised racism, prejudice and bigotry of all kinds. Probably, over the years, Muhammad and Angelo discussed the subject, albeit, perhaps not in great depth, but they were just two guys, one older and more experienced, the other, blessed with great athletic prowess, and an intelligence that far exceeded his education. So, it makes sense that they talked about racism and knew each other's feelings on the subject. The following quote, made by Ali over the years, says something important and revealing about the man: 'We have one life. It soon will be passed. What we do for God is all that will last.'

As far as Angelo was concerned, Ali's conversion to Islam made no perceptible difference to him. In a few years' time, that would change, but the only small problem for the moment was that Cassius was now Muhammad. It was a pity, as Angelo had liked the name Cassius. And, Marcellus, his middle name, was great, too. It had an Italian ring to it. But, if it was going to be Muhammad, so be it. All Angelo had to do was remember how to spell it! As for Cassius becoming a Muslim, it wasn't a big deal. Chris had married a Jewish woman. Angelo had married a Baptist. The world hadn't stopped. This was America, land of the free, which, of course, applied to religion. This was Muhammad's personal business. Angelo left the subject alone, and without giving an opinion, a lecture, or advice, he called him Muhammad and got on with the business of boxing.

Within a couple of years, the status quo had shifted. Bill Faversham had a heart attack and the congenial head of the Louisville syndicate decided to make alterations to Ali's business structure. Ali had also decided to make choices that would alter his life forever.

The syndicate's lawyer had taken over running things since Bill Faversham's heart attack, but unfortunately, he, too, became ill, and the syndicate, with Muhammad's input, decided to appoint

Dundee as the official manager. This meant that Angelo would carry on doing what he had been doing, but this time with the title of manager. Dundee had never signed a contract with the syndicate, or with Clay, now known as Ali. The conditions of their arrangement had been consummated by a handshake. Angelo's word was his bond. He trusted both the members of the syndicate and Muhammad. He always tried to do business with people he believed to be honest, which wasn't always easy in the boxing world – or in any world, come to that! He was fooled sometimes, but he tried to stick to his principle, 'If you're thinking of doing business with someone you believe is a crook, don't. Run. He's better at it than you are.'

Angelo enjoyed working with Muhammad and he was becoming truly fond of the unique, highly talented fighter. Money was never the motivating force in his life. It was a characteristic he shared with Muhammad, whose generosity and handouts are legendary. The syndicate members were no fools. They knew the value of having Angelo on their team. At the end of 1964, with Muhammad's blessing, they gave Angelo a bonus of $20,000. In 1964, that was a lot of money. Perhaps for the first time in his life, Angelo had some financial security. Of course, knowing the fight game, Angelo didn't count on anything. He tried to stay 'loose as a goose' and take things as they came, but even he was thrown a little off centre in 1966. They'd had two successful years that included a one-round KO over Sonny Liston in the return bout on 25 May 1965, exhibition bouts as far apart as Sweden and the Bahamas and a one-sided victory over Floyd Patterson on 22 November 1965 in Las Vegas. But then the syndicate's contract with Ali finished, and the deeply religious Muslim, Ali, took Herbert Muhammad as his new manager.

Dundee, as was his custom, had no contract, so even if he wanted to object to the decision, which he didn't, he had no legal case. In fact, Angelo told me that he was not upset. His life's experiences had helped mould his character. He could play the role of leader, but he was also completely at home playing the part of valued teammate. Dundee's special relationship with Ali transcended any question of an official title. Whether he was manager, co-manager, cut man, corner man or any combination of the four, he did what he had to do, to the best of his ability.

The fact that Herbert Muhammad was the son of Elijah Muhammad, leader of the Black Muslim Movement, gave the media a field day. 'Black Muslims take over'. Without a doubt, it was a racially charged time. A black religious group had taken over running the career of the world's heavyweight champion! That was news. Dundee was the only white man in Ali's entourage.

Angelo felt more than a little awkward watching Herbert call the shots but Herbert Muhammad knew the value of Dundee, and was aware of the bond that had formed between the Italian-American from South Philly, and the African-American from Louisville. To show his feelings, Herbert Muhammad bought Dundee an inscribed, custom-made diamond ring that matched the ring Muhammad Ali had given Dundee earlier in their relationship.

Things were working fine. Ali continued to beat all opposition. Throughout 1966 Muhammad defended his title successfully five times. He was a travelling champion. He beat Brian London in London on 5 August, Karl Mildenberger in Frankfurt, Germany, on 10 September and came back to the States to beat Cleveland Williams in Houston, Texas.

Whatever his religious beliefs, Muhammad Ali was still a

professional fighter, still the heavyweight champion of the world, and Angelo Dundee was still an integral part of the Ali team. Boxing was his game. His philosophy hadn't changed. All he asked was 'Could they fight?' and 'Could he make them better?' Angelo had no conflict with Ali's all-black entourage. Why would he? He was working for Muhammad Ali, not a religious movement.

However, Ali's popularity had become strong again, and his religious conversion lost most of the antagonistic response it had once. Meanwhile, as the Vietnam War took hold, there was a simmering scandal over rumours that Ali would refuse to accept the draft into the USA's armed services – and that didn't make for a hot story.

In the spring of 1967, Muhammad Ali and a talented young fighter named Jimmy Ellis who was now managed by Angelo, were in New York for their respective fights against Zora Folley and Johnny Persol, two journeymen fighters. Springtime in New York had always been an uplifting time for Angelo. Not too hot and not too cold. Flowers waking up in Central Park, trees giving the city a new look. Ali and Ellis were in high spirits. Their friendship had blossomed and their confidence was palpable. Angelo had little doubt his two fighters would be winners. He was so right. Jimmy Ellis KO'd Persol in the first round, and Muhammad Ali stopped Folley in the seventh round. Dundee, Ellis and Ali would always remember that visit to New York. The date was 22 March 1967. Muhammad Ali would not fight again until 26 October 1970.

CHAPTER 17

Exile from boxing

On 28 April 1967 in Houston, Texas, just about four weeks after his victory over Zora Folley in New York City, the governing bodies of boxing stripped Muhammad Ali of his world title for refusing to accept his military draft. On 20 June in Houston, Texas, he was convicted of draft evasion, fined $10,000, and sentenced to five years in prison. Muhammad's New York lawyer, Hayden C. Covington, immediately appealed, and Ali was allowed to stay out of jail until his appeal was resolved. That story hit every headline. The morality of the Vietnam War, the abuse by the affluent and the disproportionate amount of black men sent to Vietnam, are topics to be dealt with in another book. One remark attributed to Ali is profound. 'No Vietcong ever called me nigger.'

America was virtually divided over Ali's refusal to fight for his country. Initially, probably 70 per cent of Americans were anti-Ali. As the war progressed, and more American men were killed, the pendulum swung more in Ali's favour. For Angelo Dundee, an ex-serviceman, a former sergeant with an honourable service record, it must have been a difficult time. There was no reason to associate with Ali now. He couldn't fight in a boxing ring, and he wouldn't fight overseas for his country. Colleagues advised Angelo to forget about Ali. By the time he came back, that is *if* he came back, he'd be too old. He'd be finished. Angelo listened, but he didn't agree.

Understandably, it was a difficult situation. Angelo was a patriotic American and regardless of any political misgivings he had, he would, albeit reluctantly, have accepted his draft. Yet, deep in his heart, he understood and accepted Ali's decision. No one knew if Ali would fight again. Would he be sent to prison? It did seem the government was acting particularly hard on him. There were too many stories of sons of wealthy and influential families somehow avoiding the draft, and somehow all those families were white.

Conjecture and rumours were everywhere, and questions of right and wrong on the issue became part and parcel of everyday life in America. Why hadn't Ali volunteered to drive an ambulance or take a noncombatant job in the services? Was the government determined to break him because he was a member of the Black Muslims? And was that the reason behind boxing's governing authority stripping away his title and preventing him earning a living as a professional fighter? Muhammad didn't go to jail, and as the Vietnam War became more unpopular, Ali's principled stand became less unpopular. Angelo stoically carried on doing what he always did, working with fighters. He still had his stars – Willie Pastrano, Sugar Ramos, Luis Rodriguez and Jimmy Ellis, but he had lost his sun, Muhammad Ali.

Ali may have received some financial help from the Black Muslims. It is rumoured he had given them large amounts in the past. Money and material things were never a driving force behind

Ali's actions, but his exile from boxing went on for about two-and-a-half years, so he was likely to have had some money worries. The legal battle with the government seemed endless and costly and it's not clear who was paying for it. The cost was more than just money – it was worry, the constant pressure of not knowing if you would ever be allowed to reclaim your life. It was a difficult time.

Muhammad and Angelo were constantly in touch, mainly because of Ali's visits to the gym. He was keeping in shape, and Angelo was there for him. No questions, but always a welcoming hand of friendship. During this period, he became one of the first figures to speak out against the Vietnam War by visiting colleges all over the country. These speaking engagements helped pay his bills as did his sponsorship of the restaurant chain, 'Champburger'. His life was in turmoil but he found refuge in his religion and in the gym.

Without Ali, the heavyweight title was up for grabs. After a series of elimination bouts, Jerry Quarry, a tough Irish-American was matched against Angelo Dundee's fighter, and good friend of Ali's, Jimmy Ellis. In early April, just weeks before the scheduled world title fight, Muhammad was in Miami to do a commercial and was staying at the exclusive Four Ambassadors Hotel. He came to the gym to say 'Hi' to Angelo, watch Jimmy work out, and ask Angelo if he too could work.

'You gotta ask? The gym is yours,' Angelo told him. Then added, 'You wanna work with Jimmy?'

'That would be great, Angie. Be like old times,' Muhammad answered, smiling.

'You got it. A hundred bucks a day. Okay?'

'Hey, I don't want any money.'

'Remember,' Angelo said, his wise brown eyes looking straight at

Muhammad, 'when Jimmy sparred with you, he got paid. We gotta deal?' Angelo held out his hand.

'We gotta deal,' Muhammad said, laughing, as they shook hands.

The psychological lift to Jimmy's confidence could not be measured. He was going into the fight as a no chance long shot, but the media and odds makers didn't know about his new special sparring partner. On 27 April 1968, the Quarry–Ellis fight took place. Just before the contest, a reporter asked the same question Ali had been asked about his second fight against Henry Cooper in England. 'Is this fight Black vs. White?' Angelo and Muhammad both gave the same answer. 'Don't be childish. It's a fight between two professional boxers.'

It was a hard fought contest and there was a split decision. Two of the three judges gave the victory to the young man from Louisville. Jimmy Ellis was the new heavyweight champion of the world. Although it was a wonderful achievement for the natural middleweight to become heavyweight champion, the boxing world was divided, some still considering Ali the champion, while others backed Joe Frazier, a ferocious, non-stop puncher with a string of wins by knockout on his résumé. In fact, five states didn't recognise Ellis as the world champion. Nevertheless, by a vast majority, Jimmy Ellis was recognised as the 'Champ'.

* * *

The previous few years had been eventful for boxing and Angelo Dundee. The death of Davey Moore had eclipsed the pleasure of Sugar Ramos and Luis Rodriguez winning world titles on the same night and the joy of Willie Pastrano eventually winning the world light heavyweight title in that same year.

Willie Pastrano's retirement in 1965 left a void in Angelo's life that continued its usual pattern of highs and lows. On the plus side, as the manager/trainer of two consecutive world heavyweight champions, Ali and Ellis, he was finally getting the recognition he deserved. It was, then, no great surprise when the New York Boxing Writers voted him Boxing Manager of the Year, and presented him with the prestigious Al Buck Award, so named after the legendary sports writer.

The actual award ceremony took place at the New York Sports Writers 44th Annual Dinner in February 1969. It was a great start to the year, but if Angelo thought the remainder was going to be happy and trouble-free, he was wrong. In August, Charlie Goldman, the charismatic manager of Rocky Marciano, died. Charlie had been an inspirational mentor and friend to Angelo. What with his constant concern over Muhammad Ali's future, Angelo could have done with the wisdom and advice of a friend like Charlie Goldman.

CHAPTER 18

Back in the game

Angelo knew there was little, if anything, he could do about Ali's legal problems. All he could do was to be there for his friend if he was needed. He was deeply involved with his other fighters that he managed and on 18 April 1969, Jose Napoles fought and beat Curtis Cokes to become the world welterweight champion. Now, Angelo had two current world champions – Jimmy Ellis and Jose Naples

Angelo's seesaw fortunes continued. About 10 months later, in February 1970, Jimmy Ellis defended his title against the formidable Joe Frazier. It was a fight Dundee didn't want to take fearing Frazier would be too strong for Jimmy, but he couldn't wriggle out of it. His fears were realised. Seeing the punishment his fighter was taking, Dundee stopped the fight in round four.

Jimmy Ellis was devastated by his four round defeat by Frazier. He had never been KO'd before. He questioned Angelo about the decision to stop the fight. 'Why'd you stop me starting the fifth round? I was fine. I was only put down once.'

'You were put down twice, but you only remember once. That's why I stopped the fight,' Angelo told him.

For a manager to stop a fight is never an easy thing, nor is it easy for the referee. Angelo Dundee has his own guidelines. 'I stop a fight when, in my judgment, my guy is not capable of defending himself properly. Better I am wrong than my fighter sustains an irreparable injury. Boxing may be a tough sport, but boxers aren't gladiators who must fight to the death.'

With Ellis's defeat Angelo was down to just one world champion, Jose Napoles. He couldn't count Muhammad Ali as a champion because he wasn't permitted to box, although undoubtedly he was the people's champion. No matter, a champion has to fight.

Frazier's all-action style and heavy punching power was re-igniting an interest in boxing that had diminished since Ali had been stripped of his title. The public, more disillusioned than ever over the Vietnam War, were more sympathetic with Ali's principled stand, and felt that, until the government came to a decision on his status, he should be allowed to earn a living working at his job, and his job was fighting.

It was a complicated situation. Ali's lawyers were appealing the draft evasion conviction. So far, the conviction hadn't been upheld, and some thought there was no legal reason why Muhammad should not fight. What was needed was a State to issue Ali with a licence to box. There is no way of knowing how many States were approached, but one would have thought Nevada, home to Las Vegas, would have been interested, or California, or one of the northern, more liberal States. No. Ironically, it was a southern State, and one that had had its share of criticism from the north over its racist politics, that came through. Governor Maddox felt it was wrong and un-American to prevent a man, black or white, from earning his living and Ali got his licence.

Herbert Muhammad arranged for the former undefeated heavyweight champion to make his comeback fight against the tough Jerry Quarry in Atlanta, Georgia, on 26 October 1970. There was no question that Angelo Dundee would be part of the Ali team. The brave Quarry, as expected, fought hard, but was hopelessly outclassed and was KO'd in round three. Ali was back.

It was great news, but Frazier was now champion and Ellis warranted a return and the public wanted Ali to have a shot. In the meantime, Ali was due to fight Oscar Bonavena in November in New York and Ellis was fighting Robert Davila in Miami on Chris Dundee's promotion on 10 November. Ellis's fight was first and Angelo was there in the corner when Jimmy stopped Davila in the seventh round. Angelo realised a fight between Ali and Ellis looked inescapable. If Ali beat Bonavena, then fought Frazier and won, Ellis was next in line. If Ali lost, he would have to get by Ellis to get another shot at Frazier. Angelo had worked the corner for every Ali fight, but Ellis was his fighter, too. There was little doubt that Muhammad, even though still ring rusty after his long lay off, would be too much for Bonavena to handle, which meant an Ali–Ellis fight would be a real possibility. What corner would Dundee be in?

On 7 November 1970 Ali made his return to Madison Square Garden. Bonavena proved to be a tough and durable opponent. He was sent to the canvas three times in the 15th round, but bravely finished the fight. Ali was not his superlative best, but many thought he was still 'The Greatest'.

Angelo's worry over an Ali–Ellis fight shelved for the time being. Herbert Muhammad had arranged a fight for Ali in March 1971 against Joe Frazier for the world heavyweight championship. Fight fans across the world were caught up in the excitement of the upcoming fight. Ali was back, trying to claim his title from a fighter who didn't retreat, and had awesome power in both hands. Could Ali do it? This was a question Dundee asked himself. Frazier was not like Liston. Joe would keep throwing punches till he dropped, and then some.

It was only a four-month break for Ali after his gruelling 15-round bout against Oscar Bonavena. In those days, title fights were 15, not 12 rounds as they are now. Also, Ali's long layoff before his comeback bout against Quarry in October 1970 was only five months ago. Dundee knew how important it was for Muhammad to win back his title – that he had not lost in the ring – but he was concerned. Might it have been better for Ali to have waited a bit longer before taking on Frazier? Even the experienced Dundee couldn't be sure. You never know in boxing. Turn down a title shot? It was a tough decision.

Events were moving fast and 1971 proved to be a busy year. The Frazier–Ali bout, this first million-dollar purse fight, went 15 strength-sapping rounds. Angelo's concern had been justified. Ali was not one 100 per cent ready for a warrior like Frazier. Muhammad himself probably felt doubts subconsciously about how he would perform. For much of the fight, he grandstanded in a misguided attempt to prove how confident he was. Frazier kept coming forward and decked a tired Ali in the last round. Muhammad got up and finished the fight and proved he had a great chin, and still had the heart and courage of a lion. He lost the fight but there was better news on the horizon. On 29 June the Ali team and his millions of fans were delighted to receive the long-awaited news that the US Supreme Court had overturned Ali's draft conviction by an 8-0 vote.

Three weeks earlier, on 4 June, in Los Angeles, Jose Napoles reversed his loss on cuts, to Billie Backus, and won back his world welterweight title. For Angelo, Napoles's win helped soften the blow of Muhammad's loss to Frazier, but now, the Ali–Ellis confrontation was no longer a possibility – it was a fact. The date was set for 26 July and this development would force Angelo to make one of the most difficult decisions of his life.

It would be fair to say that Angelo's honesty and integrity were the building blocks on which the special relationship between him and Muhammad was founded. It's a bond that continues to this day. The dilemma arose over Angelo's conflict of interests. He was an important part of the Ali team, and held strong feelings of respect and affection for Muhammad. On the other hand, he had taken Jimmy Ellis from a struggling middleweight to world heavyweight champion and he had respect and affection for him, too. Angelo was deeply involved with careers of both fighters. The question was which corner would he be in on the night of the fight?

Angelo's relationship with his brother, Jimmy, hadn't diminished over the years and he continued to be the ideal big brother. He was the shoulder Angelo could lean on so Angelo called him for advice. 'As I see it, Angie,' Jimmy answered, after taking his time to digest all the information Angelo had landed on him, 'with Muhammad, you are no longer working as his manger. You are his friend, sure, and his corner man and co-trainer, but with Jimmy, you are the manager. You're the trainer, corner man and the whole bag of tricks. And you get a piece of his purse. Sure, you're his friend, too, but you gotta make a professional decision here. You're an old pro, Angie. You know your job, so you don't need me to tell you. All I'm gonna add is this. If you make a professional decision, both Jimmy and Muhammad will respect it and respect you, too.'

Before 26 July came around, both fighters knew Angelo's decision to go with Jimmy, and as Angelo's brother had predicted, both respected it. Neither fighter really wanted the bout, but there was talk of the winner getting a title shot at Joe Frazier, but whatever happened, it would be a lucrative payday. Dundee was unlikely to turn down the chance for the 31-year-old Ellis to make some good money. The boxers themselves were good friends and had sparred together on more than one occasion. There was little Dundee or Bundini Brown, Ali's corner man, could tell their respective fighters.

It was a good fight with two excellent boxers showing their considerable skills. Maybe the only ingredient lacking was passion. That's not to say the will to win was lacking in either fighter, but passion is something else. The referee stopped the fight in round 12 to prevent Ellis taking further punishment. The fighters embraced after the bout and they have remained friends until this day. Angelo's ethical dilemma was over. The fact that he had worked the corner for the less popular or prominent Ellis gave the media the opportunity to let its imagination run wild. Was there a hidden motive? Had the Black Muslims finally bullied Ali into using a black corner man, Bundini Brown, instead of Dundee? One story quoted Ali as saying, 'I'd only use Dundee again if he didn't talk so much.' All the stories were nonsense. The statement was an example of Ali's off-beat sense of humour. If Dundee didn't talk so much! How could anyone believe that the man known as the 'Louisville Lip' was being serious? Angelo was in Ali's corner for his next fight, and the fight after that, and for every fight thereafter until Muhammad Ali retired.

In 1973, Ali and Frazier took part in what became known as the 'The Bout of the Century' in which Frazier floored Ali with a left hook in the 15th round. For one reason or another, the return fight with Frazier didn't materialise at that time. Their epic confrontations were still to come. Only Herbert Muhammad and the Frazier management know why they didn't fight at that time. From Frazier's point of view it didn't work out too positively because he fought George Foreman and lost his title to that awesome opponent. Ali's chance for a title shot came in 1974, which turned out to be one of the most famous fights in the history of boxing. The now legendary fight promoter Don King got the rights to promote the Frazier–Ali fight. His inspired move was to stage the fight in Zaire, formally known as the Belgian Congo, and hype it as 'The Rumble in the Jungle'. Don King's terrific promotion and the daring concept of taking the fight to Africa played a large part in creating King's own legendary status.

What made the Foreman fight so memorable? There were so many unusual and important factors to consider. It was the first fight to be promoted by a country. The government and President Mobutu of Zaire believed that staging a world title fight of such magnitude would give the country status and credibility, as well as attracting foreign investment. They were paying $4,500,000 to be divided between Foreman and Ali, so one would assume they knew what they were doing. They did have the main key to success – a television deal. There was worldwide anticipation and excitement over this fight, which was truly unique. It wasn't being held in Las Vegas, New York or London. It was going to happen in Africa. They may have changed the name to Zaire, but to most people, it was still known by its former evocative name, the Congo.

The fight was to be held in the capital city, Kinshasa, near the mouth of the mighty Congo River. The training quarters and facilities were 40 miles away. Foreman cut his eye in training, and the fight was rescheduled from 25 September to 30 October. The Ali entourage arrived three weeks before the original fight date. The change meant they now had seven weeks in Zaire which was a long time for nerves to fray. The delay seemed to affect Foreman more than his opponent. Maybe it was the cut eye? Maybe it was the popularity of Muhammad with the local population? Maybe it was the isolation and boredom of the training camp? Whatever it was, Big George was edgy, even morose. It is hard to realise that the funny and articulate George Foreman today was considered in the early seventies to be a surly, uncommunicative, intimidating brute of a fighter. He had the same image as Sonny Liston had 10 or so years before. Both the media and the public believed he would defeat Ali, but Ali and Angelo did not. Ali told the press he would stop Foreman in eight rounds – a statement received with derision. Angelo, more cautious, believed it might take 10 or 11 rounds for Ali to stop Big George. The reporters smiled, humouring the likable corner man. The heat must have affected his judgment. Without doubt, it was turning into a memorable fight even before a punch had been thrown.

How important was the fight and its result? Well, 10 years after first winning the world heavyweight championship – the title Ali never lost in the ring but had been taken away by the Governing

Boxing Board – Ali now had an another opportunity to win it back. However, the opponent standing in his way was formidable.

Foreman had won the Olympic gold medal in 1968, eight years after Ali, then known as Cassius Clay, had won it, and George had won the heavyweight championship of the world by stopping Joe Frazier in two rounds. Joe had beaten Ali, while Big George had also destroyed Ken Norton, who had once beaten Ali. The Las Vegas bookies were making Big George a 5-2 favourite.

Foreman's fight record and awesome presence made him the media and gambling fraternity favourite, but in Zaire the people's favourites was undoubtedly Ali. Two great black fighters, both Olympic champions, both American. Why did the people of Zaire support Ali? Dr Ferdie Pecheco, who was brought into the Muhammad Ali team by Dundee and was part of the entourage in Zaire, was asked this question. 'In Kinshasa, there are more people with the name "Muhammad" or "Ali" than "George" or "Foreman",' he replied. The doctor was smart and became known on television as the 'Fight Doctor'. Some of his dogmatic medical prognostications, especially those about Muhammad Ali's Parkinson's disease, which emerged later in the fighter's life, were not met with everyone's approval or agreement. In Zaire, however, the doctor was a valued member of Ali's entourage. Along with Angelo Dundee and Gene Kilroyl, who had befriended Muhammad during his exile from boxing, Pecheco was the third white man in the entourage, which, at different times, numbered between 30 and 50 people.

The Foreman–Ali fight began with Foreman stalking the elusive Ali, whose left jab frustrated him. After three rounds Ali changed his tactics and stayed on the ropes, gloves held high, elbows tucked in while Big George pounded at the stationary figure. Angelo yelled at him to get off the ropes. This tactic became legendary, and was known as 'rope a dope'. By round seven, Forman had exhausted himself. Throwing knockout punches that landed only on arms and gloves, or into the thin air whenever Muhammad ventured into the centre of the ring, is frustrating and tiring. Before the eighth round began, Dundee told Ali to go out and finish it. He could see Foreman had nothing left. Ali, in spite of the crippling heat and humidity, somehow found the energy to do Angelo's bidding. Foreman crashed to the canvas in round eight and was unable to beat the count. Muhammad Ali had upset the odds again, and had won the world heavyweight title for the second time. What an achievement, especially given the years he had been forced out of boxing. Ali was the second fighter in history to win the heavyweight title twice. The first had been Floyd Patterson. It's a remarkable achievement for any man, but Muhammad Ali was not any man and he wasn't satisfied. He wanted more.

Muhammad Ali had many memorable fights in his long and illustrious career. His title combats with Smokin' Joe Frazier in 1971, 1974 and 1975 (The Thrilla in Manilla) were the stuff legends are made of. As for Ali's fight against Mac Foster in Tokyo, Japan, in 1972, he predicted Foster would fall in five. Foster didn't. He finished the fight, and the Japanese kept yelling at Ali, 'Taoshite Kure', which means 'Come on, sucker'. Yet another unforgettable fight in Japan took place in 1976. It's a Muhammad Ali story rarely told, which is understandable as it was a fight with the Japanese champion wrestler, Antonio Inoki, under a set of rules made from both codes. Talk about weird! It was part wrestling, part boxing.

After Inoki got nailed with some hard left jabs as he tried to grab Ali, he spent the rest of the fight on the canvas kicking Ali's legs. Seemingly, this was completely legitimate under the agreed rules of the contest. To save embarrassment all around, the judges declared the farce a draw.

On 27 September 1977, near the end of Muhammad's career, he fought one of the hardest punchers in the game. The powerful Ernie Shavers. Was he really a hard puncher? Well, in 2003 *Ring* magazine put him in the top ten greatest punchers in the history of boxing. When asked, he laughed and said, 'I don't know about that. I do know that when I hit someone they sure do see stars.'

To knock out Ali was another ball game. First of all, you had to catch him flush on the chin which was no easy task. Secondly, if you did happen to connect, it didn't mean he would be KO'd. Ken Norton had broken his jaw, and still couldn't kick him out. Nevertheless, going against Shavers looked to be a tough fight for Ali.

The fight took place at the Garden, and was being televised. It was probably the only time in television history that the commentator relayed the scoring of the judges after each round. Dundee had installed a TV set in the dressing room so the Ali team could watch the other fights on the card and soak up the hype until they had to enter the ring. Eddie Hrica, a well known matchmaker and a good pal of Angelo's, wanted to stay in the dressing room and watch the Ali fight on television. Was it because it would be a unique experience, or was it a Machiavellian plot concocted by Angelo? After each round, Eddie would run from the dressing room to the top of the ramp where Angelo could see him, and give a prearranged signal. Thumbs up if Ali had won the round, thumbs down if the judges had scored the round to Shavers, and a wave of the hand, palm down, if the round had been scored a draw. How much help was it? Well, Muhammad won the fight on points.

Any advantage for his fighter, no matter how small, how borderline or controversial, Angelo grabbed with both hands. One could argue that just having Angelo in your corner was like having an extra fist. In all those memorable and unusual fights, Dundee was there, with Muhammad, and he was there for the most memorable fight of all.

CHAPTER 19

A new star dazzles

1974 had been a memorable a year for Ali and Dundee. A little like 1964, when Ali, then known as Cassius Clay, had beaten Sonny Liston to win the heavyweight title. Now, at the beginning of 1975, as Muhammad began training to defend his title against Chuck Wepner on 24 March, he thought it unbelievable that once again he was the heavyweight champion of the world. The event was covered by the media worldwide and the name Muhammad Ali was being heralded across the nations.

In 1975, another young talented amateur boxer won a title. He became the Amateur Athletic Union (AAU) welterweight champion. This was a big event for an 18-year-old boy from Wilmington, North Carolina. In fact, for him and his family, it was probably far more memorable than Ali beating Foreman. How did that young man feel when he won the AAU championship again the following year? He won a gold medal at the Pan-American Games, too, which was quite an achievement However, his sights were set on an even bigger target. His aim was perfect. It was his crowning glory. At the 1976 Olympics in Montreal he won the junior welterweight Gold medal. The charismatic Ray Charles Leonard had arrived on the world's stage.

Even before his first professional fight, there was a buzz about the newcomer. Although he and Muhammad were a long way apart in weight and age, there were similarities that were identifiable. Both were good looking – movie star looks in fact. It was difficult to decide who was the more charming when they turned it on, and their sense of humour, though different, was part of their character. Dedicated to training to the point of fanaticism, both had superlative skills, and as Leonard's career progressed, he showed the same ability to take a punch and an equal reserve of courage in adversity as Muhammad.

They certainly liked the ladies. However, their different backgrounds and ages accounted for their different reactions to racism. Ray didn't have that deep-rooted anger towards bigots as Ali did. That's not to say Ray didn't loath racism, because he did, but he took it for what it was, stupid ignorance. Ray also had a different upbringing to Ali and he grew up in a different time. His ambitions lay in the arts and education, not in boxing. Music was his and his mother's passion. That may explain why his mom named him after singer Ray Charles. The Sugar got tagged on as respect to the legendary Sugar Ray Robinson.

He was fortunate to have been represented from the very beginning by a no-nonsense businessman. Mike Trainer was a lawyer with both his feet on the ground, with a practice in Silver Springs, Maryland. He had the talent and confidence to cross swords with any high-priced New York 'legal eagle' if necessary, but more importantly, he had Leonard's best interests at heart. Leonard was probably aware of this as he had an instinctive sense of who was genuine and who was phoney. It's an instinct Leonard never lost, just as he never lost his respect for education and the corporate world. Even in his youth, Leonard decided that being represented by a smart, honest lawyer was the right way to go. If Leonard had thought Mike Trainer other than 'smart' and 'honest', he would not have become involved with him in the first place. Sugar Ray knew what he wanted. If he felt he was not being represented properly, he would not think twice about making changes – Sugar Ray Leonard was not only tough in the ring – although his iron will was often hidden beneath his unquestionable charm.

Since his amateur days, Sugar Ray Leonard had worked with his trainer, Dave Jacobs, and former insurance man and close personal friend, Janks Morton. It had been Janks who had recommended Mike Trainer to Ray. It was a small, tight-knit group all dedicated to making Ray Leonard a champion. Their problem was they knew very little about professional boxing. However, they knew enough to know that Ray needed a manager who did.

* * *

After his triumphant victory over George Foreman, Ali, with Dundee in his corner, toured the world taking on all challengers. He won every fight, including reversing his defeat by Smokin' Joe Frazier in 1971, in a bout known as 'The Thriller in Manila' held in 1975, that rivalled his epic 'Rumble in the Jungle' confrontation with Foreman a year earlier. Also in 1975 he won his fight against Wapner in the fading minutes of the 15th round. There were also two ferocious bouts against Ken Norton, a loss and a win, that were close enough to cause controversy, and argument, among fight fans to this day. These strength-sapping fights naturally took their toll on a man in his 30s and a price would eventually be paid.

It was at the April 1976 championship fight against Jimmy Young in Landover, Maryland that Angelo first met the not-yet-famous amateur from Wilmington. Ray, who was a big fan of Ali, had come to the fight with a couple of other members of the USA Olympic Boxing Team, hoping to meet his hero. After he informed one of the stewards that he was in the Olympic boxing team, Ray was permitted to go back to the dressing room area. Ali and Dundee had an inbuilt affection for young fighters, as the youngster was about to find out. He was allowed to stay for a few minutes while Ali warmed up – Dundee always had his fighters get a slight sweat on to loosen their muscles before they entered the ring – and they talked boxing, mainly about the upcoming summer Olympics in Montreal.

Muhammad arranged for Ray and a couple of other members of the boxing team to be moved to better seats. Ray, full of excitement, went to find his team-mates and tell them that he had actually had a conversation with Muhammad Ali and they were going to sit in the really expensive seats. Wow! What a night it was turning out to be. To top it off, Ali also arranged for Ray, along with another member of the Olympic boxing team, to take a bow from the ring. The young Olympians didn't mind too much that the Ali–Young fight was pretty bad. Ray Leonard has remained an Ali fan to this day.

Later in the year, at a party in New York, the three men met up again. Ray, now the recipient of the 1976 junior welterweight Olympic gold medal, humbly accepted Angelo's congratulations. After the three brothers in sport had chatted for a moment about the big impact the USA boxing team had made, Ray mentioned he was thinking of turning professional and was looking for a manager. Muhammad told him, 'If you want a good manager, here's Angelo.' All three men smiled and Angelo nodded his head benignly and said nothing. The moment passed, but as events turned out, it wasn't forgotten, at least not by Ray Leonard.

Within six or seven weeks after Muhammad's prophetic remark, Angelo Dundee became the manager of Sugar Ray Leonard. It all began with a phone call to Dundee's office. Betty Mitchell, Dundee's efficient long-time office manager, answered and quickly ascertained who was calling and why. Before putting the call through to Angelo, she put the call on hold and informed him: 'It's a Mike Trainer. He's a lawyer from Silver Springs, in Maryland. He says he represents the Olympic champion, Sugar Ray Leonard. Do you want to speak to him?' Dundee hesitated. He didn't know a Mike Trainer. Sure, he knew young Ray Leonard, but what did his lawyer want? The remark Muhammad had made to Ray recommending him as a manager didn't enter his mind.

'Okay, put him through,' Angelo said as he picked up his phone.

After the polite introductions, Trainer began explaining that as Ray Leonard's lawyer, he had formed a corporation to look after Ray's financial interests and he was looking around for the right fight manager for Sugar Ray. Was Angelo interested? An Olympic champion! Of course he was interested. However, Dundee was busy working with Muhammad, and Jimmy Ellis was still getting fights, so he had reservations. He had liked the youngster on the two occasions they had met, and it was a big plus that Ray was already popular with the American public. Dundee affirmed his interest, they discussed his involvement, and by early November, the no-

nonsense Mike Trainer had sent Angelo a draft contract to act as Leonard's personal representative, boxing advisor, and manager for a six-year period. Dundee would receive 15 per cent of Leonard's earnings from boxing. There is no information on any other points, clauses, or conditions of the contract, but Dundee is no lover of signing contracts and would rather deal with someone he trusts on a handshake.

He didn't know Trainer well enough to tell whether he could trust him or not. Could he have gotten a better deal? Maybe. Should he have talked it over with Chris before signing? For sure. Angelo's strength was never in his business acumen. Trainer was a tough cookie and Angelo, as we have learned, has a compassionate and non-confrontational nature. He agreed to go to Silver Springs to finalise the deal. The welcome he received from Mike Trainer was cordial and he had arranged accommodation for the night at a comfortable hotel. They would discuss business in the morning after breakfast.

The meeting took place in Trainer's office. Besides Trainer, the other participants were Dave Jacobs, Ray's trainer; Janks Morton, a friend and adviser; Ray's father; and Ray Leonard himself. It was a pleasant meeting and Trainer agreed with Angelo that as Ray had a good family relationship, it would be wise for him to have a home base. In the emotional and demanding sport of professional boxing, a loving family home life can give security and keep a young fighter's feet on the ground. There seemed to be agreement all round, and a sense of excitement and anticipation filled the room. Doubts left Dundee's head. He could see these were all good people. No need to sweat over every dot in the contract. It wasn't Dundee's style to ask for more for himself – for his fighters, of course, but not for himself. Many managers took 40 or even 50 per cent of their fighter's purse. Dundee took 30 per cent from Jimmy Ellis. It would have made sense if he had asked for a sliding scale of percentages. For example, if with Dundee's influence, Leonard started making over $1,000,000 a fight, Dundee should get at least 20 per cent. Two hundred thousand is a lot of money to pay someone, but not if that someone has helped you make $800,000 for yourself. It's unlikely that Chris Dundee would have accepted the deal as is was. Angelo was a different kind of person. He was someone who, because of his unique personality, could fit comfortably into the lives of such complicated, talented and charismatic athletes as Ali and Leonard. On 16 November 1976, Angelo Dundee signed the contract that made him the manager of Sugar Ray Leonard.

CHAPTER 20

More mountains to climb

Within a short time of signing the contract, Dave Jacobs, Janks Morton and Sugar Ray were in Miami at the Fifth Street Gym where Ray was training under Angelo's scrutiny. Angelo wanted to evaluate the young Olympian and watched Ray working out. There was no doubt he had talent and was in good shape, but he would need to build up his stamina. It was a slightly unusual experience for Dundee. He was the manager, but not the trainer. That was Dave Jacob's job.

Ray's first fight was set for 5 February 1977, giving the Leonard team around two months to prepare for a six-round bout. This would be a big leap from the three-round limits for amateur bouts Ray was used to, and happy with. Getting Ray ready for an extra three rounds was Dave's responsibility. Selecting opponents was Dundee's responsibility. He did it well. He was insistent that Leonard be brought along slowly. Ray's first opponent was Puerto Rican Luis Vega, and the venue was the Civic Center, Baltimore, Maryland. Leonard won the six-round fight by unanimous decision. He was off to a winning start.

The fight was promoted by ABC-TV and Leonard was paid

$40,000, a record at the time for a boxer's professional debut. The thinking behind ABC's promoting the fight was that the popular Leonard would take over from the ageing Ali as the fans' favourite. Of course, in reality, no one would or could replace Ali, but the time was ripe for a new fighting hero. That year, Ali had had two hard fights that went the full 15 rounds. These demanding bouts were beginning to take their toll on him.

Sugar Ray had five fights in 1977 and had won them all, four by a knock-out. By February 1978, he was fighting eight-round bouts. Dundee wanted him fighting ten-round bouts by the summer, provided, of course, that Angelo thought that Ray would win.

Muhammad Ali was getting ready to defend his title over 15 rounds against a puffed up light heavyweight, former Olympic champion, Leon Spinks. Angelo believed there was only one opponent Muhammad had to worry about: Mr Old Age.

The upcoming Ali title defence against Leon Spinks occupied a chunk of Dundee's thoughts and time. That is not to say Angelo put Ray Leonard's career on hold. The February fight, held at the Civic Center in Baltimore, was where Ray, in his first eight-round contest, won a unanimous decision over Rocky Ramon, which showed the progress he was making. Dundee gave credit to Dave Jacobs and Janks Morton for keeping Ray in great shape. Whether or not they gave Dundee credit for assiduously selecting Ray's opponents, there is no way of knowing. The team was winning, and as far as Dundee was concerned, that's what counted.

That Leonard had become a recognizable name in so short a time was no accident. Tying in to ABC-TV had been a big plus, but the fact that Leonard was represented by Angelo Dundee, the best known and most successful boxing figure outside the ring in

America, was an even biggger plus. He was the man who handled two heavyweight world champions – Ali, then Ellis – who reigned one after the other. Dundee was 'The Man'. He was the guy who had had another two world champions, Luis Rodriguez and Sugar Ramos, crowned champions on the same night! And hadn't he represented Willie Pastrano and Jose Napoles, who had been champion in 1969, lost it and then won it again in 1971? That Angelo Dundee was something else and the media knew he was always good for a story. And, of course, Angelo knew from experience how to relate to the press. Many of the leading sports writers were friends of his. And it didn't do any harm that Ray was good looking, had a great sense of humour, was modest and a fine talker. His popularity was growing as fast as his bank account. All he had to do was to keep on winning.

Unlike Ali, Ray wasn't the type to give his money away. He was strong willed, and like Ali, he was far more amenable to suggestions than to instructions or orders. But he always listened. Ray was certainly nobody's fool, but because Ray had his old trainer Dave Jacobs and adviser and friend Janks Morton with him constantly, it was difficult for Dundee and Leonard to bond in the same way that Dundee had with Ali. Ali and Dundee had had that early training period in Miami Beach when they had time to really get to know each other without the complication of other people intruding on what was the driving force of both their lives – the fight game in general, and Ali's career in particular. Angelo understood that Muhammad was a one-off situation. He hoped that he and Ray would grow closer as time went by. Ray liked and respected Angelo but was cautious with his praise, not wanting to sow seeds of envy in Dave Jacobs.

Dundee was glad Jacobs was doing such a good job and he didn't feel any guilt when he began to concentrate fully on the Ali–Spinks fight set for 15 February. Ali hadn't fought for five months, and getting back to training had proved difficult. He wasn't 'juiced up' for the fight. Spinks was no Foreman, no Frazier. He'd won an Olympic gold medal, but he'd had little professional experience. True, he was a very good boxer, but he was no match for the world champion. Ali couldn't get excited about this fight and didn't take it seriously. He should have.

* * *

It's a hell of an achievement to win the world heavyweight title. To win it twice, phenomenal! It had never been won three times, but that is what Muhammad Ali had to do. He had to because the underrated Leon Spinks, a fighter Ali had hardly bothered to train for, had beaten him; Spinks had taken his title.

Now for the inquest! Was Ali finished? Had he lost his desire to win? Was he just a shadow of the Ali of old? The press posed the question of Ali's retirement. The public agreed. But Ali had other ideas. Far from hanging up his gloves, he immediately began planning how he could get that title for an unprecedented third time. Dundee knew Ali would work to get back his strength and retire as the champion. He believed Muhammad was as motivated now as he had ever been. Dundee, who had been there on that memorable night in 1964 and again in 1974, had no doubt his fighter would make it happen. And, Angelo would be there, as usual, working Ali's corner.

The return bout was set for 15 September 1978, in New Orleans. For Muhammad, it was a fight that ranked as importantly as any of his previous confrontations. If he lost, it would probably be the end of his career. The call to retire would be overwhelming. However, if he won, he would make sporting history. Angelo was immersed in the preparations for the title fight and the build up was beginning to get to him. Fortunately, over in the Leonard camp, Ray had won a couple of 10-round bouts and things looked good. At least they did, until Angelo received a letter from Mike Trainer. After he had read it, he felt like he'd been hit in the solar plexus with a hard left hook. The letter was dated 8 August 1978.

Angelo re-read it and still didn't believe it. He handed it to his office manager, Betty Mitchell. As she read it, she chose certain passages to speak out loud with her added commentary. 'What does he mean by writing, "I'm concerned by the lack of time and effort you've put into Sugar Ray"? How dare he say this, "As the second highest paid person in the organization, we all expected more. To date, your involvement has consisted of arriving approximately two days before a fight, meeting with the press, and working Ray's corner at fight time".'

Betty read on, and Angelo sat in his leather swivel chair bewildered. After Betty had finished, she exclaimed, 'He's got to be crazy! What does he expect you to do?' The answer to that question was spelled out in the letter. Trainer, in classic 'lawyer-speak', had written, 'I want to adjust your compensation so that it is more in line with your duties.'

As far as can be ascertained, there was no reason Dundee had to agree to Trainer's demand. Dundee had a signed contract. That must have meant something. Angelo was personally hurt and humiliated. He knew his value, and what he contributed – after all, Leonard was fighting 10-round bouts now, and hadn't lost a fight.

Not to detract from Ray's talent, but fighting the right opponent, at the right time, is a crucial factor in winning contests. The big credibility input of being managed by Dundee was difficult to put a price on, and having perhaps the best corner man of his time working your corner could sometimes be the difference between victory and defeat. Guys in the fight game understood these things. Angelo never had any problems with Cuco Conde, Whitey Esnault, Joe Netro, Ernesto Chorales or Herbert Muhammad. They were fight men.

On the other hand, Mike Trainer was a businessman and a lawyer, too. Whether he felt justified or not, if he could get Dundee cheaper, that was the way to go. As others have said on many occasions, 'It's business, nothing personal.' But for Angelo, it was personal. For a man with the personal warmth of an Italian-American, Angelo found Trainer to be a cold fish and would probably admit that perhaps he tried too hard to be friendly with Trainer in an attempt to keep a convivial atmosphere in the camp. Who knows if Trainer was even aware of Dundee's efforts? Maybe he took it as the actions of someone trying to pull a fast one, or maybe as a sign of weakness. One fact seems inescapable. If Dundee took less, someone else would get more.

If Trainer, or even Leonard, had any legitimate quarrel with Dundee's work performance the period around the second week in February, when Ali fought – and lost his title to – Spinks, and the period around the first couple of weeks in September would have given their argument some validity. 15 September was the date of the return fight between Ali and Spinks and quite simply, Angelo couldn't be in two different places at once.

Angelo's anger and feelings of bewilderment had subsided, and he concentrated on something more important to him than a potential loss of dollars – Muhammad trying to win his title back. On 15 September, in New Orleans, after 15 rounds of boxing, the judges gave their decision. Once again, Muhammad Ali was champion of the world. The achievement was overwhelming. The first man to win the title three times! A record was set that would live forever in the annals of boxing history. It would take a fighter of extraordinary skills in an incredible set of circumstances for it ever to be broken.

For the next 24 hours, Dundee was in a fog of emotions. Pride was uppermost, both in Muhammad, and to a lesser degree in himself. The joy of the occasion was tempered a little by Muhammad's announcement that he was going to finally retire from boxing. He had made that announcement before in the past. This time, Angelo and millions of fight fans regrettably agreed with Muhammad's decision. Angelo, fearing for his friend's future health hoped that this time, Muhammad really meant it.

As for the contractual dispute with Mike Trainer, Dundee's lawyers were now handling it and Angelo got on with doing his job as Ray's manager. During the Ali–Spinks fight period, he had been unavailable for Ray, and he had arranged with his trusted friend, Eddie Hrica to arrange fights for Ray. Strangely enough, Trainer, when notified by Angelo, had no problem with the temporary arrangement. Of course, Dundee had to give his approval to any decision but he was only a phone call away.

The arrangement worked pretty well, except for one time when a bout had been arranged with the big, tough boxer named Tommy 'Hit Man' Hearns before Dundee passed it, and it was a fight he didn't want. The chosen opponent was big and strong. It wasn't that Angelo thought Ray couldn't win, but it would be a hard fight.

Why take a chance so early in his career? The two fighters had previously sparred together in the gym and it became too serious, resulting in a little bad blood between them. Dundee didn't want Ray in a needle fight with a tough youngster who was three or more inches taller. There was plenty of time for wars. Easy does it. The more fights Ray won, the more his reputation as a winner would grow. As Dundee said, 'Like Sonny Liston, Ray is wrapping himself in a cloak of invincibility, which in itself can psyche out an opponent before a blow is thrown. And this time, there ain't gonna be a Cassius Clay to strip it away.'

At Dundee's insistence, the bout was taken out, although the two fighters would meet eventually. It would be down the road when they fought to decide who would become the undisputed welterweight champion of the world. Some of the media guys wrote that Ray was ducking Hearns. Sensibly, that's exactly what he was doing. Under the generalship of Angelo Dundee, Ray was going to fight the battle on his own terms in his own time. In the meantime, as long as the two boxers kept winning, the interest in an eventual confrontation would only grow. For those who wonder about the impact a good coach makes to a fighter's career, that example of knowing when to pass on a specific opponent at certain times says it all. If Sugar Ray Leonard had fought Tommy Hearns too early and lost, he may never have had his magnificent career. From September 1978 to the end of the year, Ray had four fights. That's one a month, and he won them all.

In February 1979, Ray was fighting in Miami Beach on a Chris Dundee promotion. To date, Ray had gone 17 fights without a loss, beating fighters of the calibre of Johnny Gant, Randy Shields and Floyd Mayweather, Sr. He was featured on NBC's televised fights and his popularity was growing exponentially. A title fight was in the foreseeable future. Mike Trainer had accompanied Ray to Miami, and he and Angelo had a chance to talk. The meeting was pleasant enough, but Trainer and Dundee were as different as chalk and cheese – they came at the situation from entirely different perspectives. Dundee may well have been the fight manager and the expert on the fight game, but Trainer was a lawyer and businessman and it was he who dealt with Leonard's TV contracts. As a compromise, a new contract acceptable to Angelo would be arranged. Trainer was learning the business side of the fight game fast and it would seem he had already learned what buttons to push to manipulate Angelo.

As far as Ray and Angelo getting along personally, there didn't seem to be any problems. There seemed to be a bond developing between them. Angelo's affinity for young, aspiring fighters made him a good and sympathetic listener to the intelligent Leonard. Without prying, Angelo learned of Ray's early days. Although Ray had been a success in the amateurs, he hadn't had the intention of pursuing a career as a professional fighter. His father became ill and he wanted to help his family financially, and Ray realised that as Olympic champion, he had the key to making some quick money. Ray's inclination was to obtain a good education, then perhaps look for an opportunity in some musical or other artistic endeavour.

There was no doubt he had the brains and determination to succeed in almost any field he put his mind to. Like other great athletes before him, the thrill of competing and the respect and admiration his superb talent got him, slowly became addictive. Fame, wealth and adoration mixed together make a potent drug. That heady cocktail was about to get even stronger. Ray was to realise his first major goal. In Las Vegas on 30 November 1979 he fought Wilfredo Benitez, the WBA (World Boxing Association) champion. It was an excellent contest between two well-matched boxers. In the 15th and final round, Benitez succumbed to his stronger opponent. Sugar Ray Leonard was the new welterweight champion of the world.

Naturally, there was elation and celebrations in the Leonard camp, and no one would have guessed of the conflict beneath the surface. Though the contractual dispute did not seem to affect Trainer or Ray, Dundee was emotionally involved. He still felt embarrassed and humiliated. Angelo's confidence was not strong and he would have been hurt to find out that Ray didn't think highly of him, both as a person and as a fight manager.

The contractual problem was still being negotiated, lawyer-to-lawyer, when they reached and passed 1980. The latest clause inserted in the new compromise contract by Mike Trainer of behalf of Sugar Ray Leonard, Inc, the corporation Trainer had formed for Ray at the very start of their relationship, was that Angelo would work on a fight–to–fight basis, and would receive his 15 per cent as long as Leonard chose to have him work in his corner. The years left on the contract would become null and void. Why didn't Dundee discuss the matter with Ray directly? Angelo did receive a letter from Trainer stating that Ray expressly requested that the problems be resolved directly between Trainer and Dundee, but it seems likely that Angelo did not relish a confrontation with Ray. Maybe Angelo didn't want to learn if Ray, who obviously knew all about the matter, was really calling the shots. It was something Angelo didn't want to believe as he genuinely liked Sugar Ray and thought the feeling was mutual. Besides, and perhaps more importantly, they were still winning fights. There were greater triumphs to be won. Why rock the boat?

In March 1980, Sugar was defending his WBC world title against Dave 'Boy' Green, a good British boxer. Once again, a big fight was being held at the Civic Center in Landover, Maryland, and for the Leonard camp, it was a big fight, not only because it was a title defence, but if Ray was successful, a fight against the legendary Roberto Duran was waiting in the wings. Ray was in great shape. He and Angelo would think about Duran later. 'First,' Angelo said, 'let's take care of Green.'

The mood in the dressing room before the fight was positive and oozed confidence. Green was good, but knowledgeable fight fans, even supportive British ones, knew Leonard was in a class above. Ray, Angelo, Janks Morton, Mike Trainer, and his partner, Jim Ryan, were in the warm dressing room permeated with the smells of liniment and oils. There wasn't a lot of time left before Dundee and Morton would escort Leonard into the arena. Ray was relaxed. He had gone through his warm-up routine and his body glistened with sweat. Dundee smiled. Ray had that same devotion to training as the young Muhammad Ali.

According to Angelo, at that point and without any preamble Mike Trainer produced a hand-written contract and asked him to sign it. Everyone in the room encouraged Angelo to do so. Trainer, who was particularly friendly, pointed out that it would be in Angelo's best interest to sign. He would still get his 15 per cent. The only change from the original contract was its duration. Hadn't Angelo always said that the most important thing was for the fighter to have faith in his manager? Well, Trainer pointed out Angelo must know Ray had great faith, as well as admiration, and affection for him. What else did he need? This hand-written contract would solve everything. Angelo signed it. There were hugs and handshakes all around. Everyone was happy, including Angelo. Enveloped in the warm, brotherly feeling, the gladiator and his sword carriers left the room for the roped-in battlefield. The only one who wasn't happy was Dave 'Boy' Green – he got KO'd in round four.

When Dundee told Betty Mitchell and his lawyer what had transpired, two more people were not happy. Betty told him he had lost three years on his old contract and that he had been coerced. He should sue. His lawyer told him that he'd been a fool to sign any contract without legal advice. Did he wish to start proceedings? Of course Angelo said no. It wasn't his style. Was it foolishness or wisdom? Dundee knew he shouldn't have signed a legal document without a lawyer, but it's possible he didn't really care. All Angelo was losing was future earnings. If after two years, Ray decided he no longer needed him, so? If Ray decided he didn't want to fight any more, so? Dundee wouldn't exactly be on the bread line. He was currently the only non-boxing personality in the fight game known to the public other than Don King. Dundee could make big paydays through speaking engagements. He turned down offers every week. And how long would it take for him to tie into another contender or champion? Not long, not long at all. He was the man who helped make Ali a superstar. Fighters sought him out. He didn't even have to look. Sugar Ray Leonard was now a champion, but hadn't yet reached his full potential. That's why it's probable that Dundee, being the kind of man he was, didn't lose any sleep over a contract that potentially earned him less money than originally agreed to. Angelo wanted to be a part of Ray's future. He wanted to be in the corner when Ray met Roberto Duran. He wanted to be in the corner if and when Ray eventually fought Tommy Hearns. That's what Dundee was all about. He needed approval, appreciatiation and respect. Angelo was far more affected by the thought that perhaps Trainer and Leonard did not have respect and appreciation him than he was about money. It was about the pride and glory of playing a part in a victory for his fighter. That trumped extra dollars in his pocket. Not he in Ray's corner for the Roberto Duran fight? It would probably not have been hard to have talked Angelo into doing the job for nothing!

CHAPTER 21

No mas, no mas!

It was a great night in Montreal. On 20 June 1980, Sugar Ray Leonard was back at the Olympic Stadium where he had won a gold medal. The stadium was packed. Not only was Sugar Ray defending his welterweight title, he was also defending it against the former lightweight world champion – now a fully fledged welterweight – the iconic Roberto Duran. It was expected to be an exciting fight. It was. It has happened many times in boxing, a slugger comes out intending to box, but after a couple or more rounds of getting hit, the blood rushes to his head and he reverts to slugging. It was a little like that for Leonard against Duran, except Leonard wasn't a slugger. He was a boxer who could punch.

Dundee wanted Ray to dance, jab and keep off the ropes. That was the fight plan. It was Dundee himself who said that Duran had three great weapons – one left hand, one right hand, and one head. He warned Ray not to fight Roberto's fight. Fortunately for Duran the bout was fought at close quarters in the corners and against the ropes, where the tough, former Panama street kid, out-mauled the usually elusive Leonard. It was no surprise when Duran took a majority decision. Leonard lost his unbeaten record along with his world welterweight title. The only consolation Ray had was there would be a return fight in around five months' time.

Dave Jacobs, Ray's trainer, was conspicuous by his absence. This had been the case for many months. Without any histrionics, Ray and Dave had fallen out, and Janks Morton took over as trainer. Notwithstanding the loss to Duran, there was no doubting Ray's fitness. Janks had learned quickly and was doing a good job.

The return fight with Duran was going to take place in New Orleans on 25 November 1980. Dundee had no worries about Ray being in shape. Janks was taking care of that, but a new fight plan was of equal importance. The plan was to give him continual practice moving off the ropes, where Duran's bruising style was effective, and keep the fight in the centre of the ring where Ray could move laterally. Ray would frustrate Duran by making him miss, then counter with either hand. Ray's superior hand speed was going to be a great advantage, providing he stayed off the ropes.

Duran was similar to Liston in some ways: rough, tough and a better boxer than he was given credit for. Both had an arrogance and self-confidence that demoralised opponents. At a meeting, just before their first bout in Montreal, Roberto's insulting and dismissive behaviour towards Leonard and his wife, Juanita, had made Ray lose his cool. The insults had been made for a reason – to make Ray's temper override his brains in the ring. It had worked and Ray had lost the fight. However, this one would be different. Ray would use psychological warfare. Before a fight, Duran never shaved, making him look even meaner than he was. Angelo had a plan. They would make fun of the unshaved Roberto and show their contempt for him. At the 'weigh-in' Angelo and Ray arrived, sporting false beards.

Roberto and his entourage couldn't believe their eyes, but they immediately got the message. As he and Dundee had planned, Ray treated Duran and his team with the utmost contempt, and acted with an arrogance never seen before from the usually quiet and well-mannered young man. Ray would whisper something to Angelo, then they would both look over at Duran and chuckle at their secret joke. Another weapon Dundee included in his plan to undermine Duran's mental attitude was having Ray 'bulk up' a little. There was no doubt the Duran team noticed that Leonard looked bigger and stronger. That was probably the reason that after the weigh-in, Duran, contrary to the practice of most professional fighters, went to a restaurant and ate to excess. Doing that would come back to haunt him. This mind game Dundee had come up with was not in any fight manager's instruction book, but then Dundee was not a run-of-the-mill manager. People like Mike Trainer didn't understand that.

For the first seven rounds of the fight, Sugar Ray kept to his plan, negating all Duran's bullish attacks. Duran was the hunter and he stalked the elusive prey. Every time he took a shot, the prey had moved. Duran began to burn with frustration. What was even more frustrating for Duran was that the prey was hitting back, and leaving before he could respond. The eighth round began and Ray, now in control, taunted Duran by pretending to throw a bolo punch. He stood in front of the 'bull from Panama', showing his contempt, defying him to hit him. Duran moved forward, changed his mind, turned his back on Leonard, raised his arms and walked back to his corner to the astonishment of everyone. The fight was over.

Technically, Duran should have been disqualified, but the official result was a win for Leonard by knock out. He was once again the WBC, welterweight champion of the world.

A question mark hangs over the fight to this day. Some fight fans, and a few media people, thought it was a fake and that the fight had been thrown. When Duran turned his back on Sugar Ray and walked back to his corner, most fight fans believe Duran called out, '*No mas, no mas*' ('No more, no more') though he claims to have said '*No quiero pelear con el payaso*' (I do not want to fight with this clown') before going on to say '*No mas*'. There is also a belief that gorging himself with food after the weigh-in led to stomach cramps during the fight.

In 1981, because there were two world boxing sanctioning bodies, the World Boxing Association, and the World Boxing Council, there were two welterweight champions of the world: WBC champion Sugar Ray Leonard and the WBA champion, Tommy Hearns. Duran was no quitter, or a coward. His long, successful record proved that. No doubt, the way Leonard frustrated him played a part in the decision he made, and whether or not he actually said '*no mas, no mas*,' it was for all intents and purposes no more, no more to his career.

*   *   *

Leonard's victory over Roberto Duran added to Angelo Dundee's Christmas celebrations. Angelo loved it all: the food, the presents, being with his family. How blessed he was. That evening, as he sat quietly in his den, the kids asleep in bed, Helen in the sitting room watching television, he smoked a cigar and thought about his brother Jimmy.

They had managed to spend a little time together in New Orleans in November. Jimmy had been there for the fight. It had been great seeing him, but it left Angelo with a nagging worry about his brother's health. Nothing he could pin down: just something about him. When Angelo asked him if he was okay, Jimmy assured him he was fine. He said he'd been having a little gas, that's all. Nevertheless, it made Angelo uneasy. He tried not to think negative thoughts. Hadn't Jimmy often told him worrying don't change a thing? Jimmy was right, of course.

Putting down his cigar, Angelo got up from the comfortable, leather armchair, went to his desk and took out the letter Sugar Ray had sent. Once back in his armchair Angelo re-read what Ray had sent to Helen and him before the Wilfredo Benitez fight, about a year ago when the contractual problem with Mike Trainer was getting to him. Ray had spent some time with the Dundees in Miami. The note always lifted Angelo's spirits. It showed that hard work, doing what is right, doesn't always go unnoticed and things do work out for the best. The note read: 'Hello buddies. Just a few lines to say things are going well and I am very happy to say that not only have I found the world's greatest manager and wife, but two dynamite friends. Love ya! The next world champion, Sugar Ray.'

No doubt about it, Ray had enjoyed his time in Miami Beach. He was popular with the guys at the gym, but they kept their girlfriends away. Not that Ray would flirt with a buddy's girlfriend, but he was girl magnet. He would turn heads as he walked down Lincoln Road, or hang out at the Coconut Grove Marina, wearing his white pants and black polo shirt. He was a cool dude. Besides his strict training regimen, Ray went deep-sea water fishing or played golf. Everyone who met him liked this charming, well-mannered young man. Those who got to know him soon appreciated his sense of humour. Having a sense of humour was part of the cement that bonded Ray and Muhammad with Angelo. Being able to laugh together is important.

He remembered a story about Sugar Ray playing golf, the other two being a former mayor, who shall remain nameless, and a bombastic, big shot who happened to be a terrible golfer. During the game, he watched with envy the young black man who had only played a few games, hitting the ball like a pro. In fact, the most time Ray had spent on a golf course was for training purposes. It was a place to run and sprint. The big shot began making a couple of tasteless remarks about how blacks had a natural rhythm from listening to the drums in Africa. And wasn't it a pity they hadn't developed their intellect more? Negroes in many ways were a like racehorses bred for sport. D'you know what I mean? The former mayor was embarrassed and uttered, 'Come on. Let's play golf for chrissakes.'

Ray ignored the remarks and began hitting the ball longer and straighter, infuriating Mr Big Shot further. At the finish of the game, won by Ray, while they were having a drink at the nineteenth hole surrounded by club members, Mr Big Shot asked Ray if he could give him any tips on his game. Ray nodded thoughtfully as the members crowded in closer to hear his words of wisdom.

'Well, if I was you,' Ray began thoughtfully, 'I would cut about five, no, make that six or seven inches off the bottom of your clubs.' There was a hush in the room. The members wanted to hear more.

Mr Big Shot asked, 'You mean cut six or seven inches off my driver, right?'

'I mean all your clubs,' Ray answered seriously.

'All! Do you really think that will improve my game?'

'No,' Ray said, laughing, 'but it sure would make it easier for you to throw them in the trash bag. Man, you're bad. Real bad.'

There was a nanosecond of complete silence, then the room burst into laughter. Even the embarrassed Mr Big smiled. He had to look a good sport in front of the club's members.

'Very funny. You got me.' Mr Big Shot said. 'Say, Ray, when are you going to fight Tommy Hearns?'

'We're talking about maybe in a year or two.'

'Hey, Ray, don't you know – you can run but you can't hide? I guess you'll have to fight him sometime, probably in Vegas, right?'

Ray shrugged.

'I'll be there,' the man continued, 'and can you guess who I'll be betting on?'

'Tommy Hearns,' Ray said, grinning.

'You bet your sweet ass. I may not be a hotshot golfer, but I sure know how to pick a winner.' He had got his shot in.

Ray smiled and said, 'We'll see, we'll see.'

Years later, in the mid-nineties, when asked on a video interview about the golfing story in Miami, Ray couldn't remember it. Were they sure it wasn't Tiger Woods? No, they understood it was Sugar Ray Leonard. Ray answered by saying if it hadn't been him, he certainly wished it had.

Angelo put Ray's letter and past memories away. It was nearing time to concentrate on the job at hand. In March 1981 Ray had a warm-up fight, another in June. Neither fight was a walkover. He wanted good opponents not deadbeats. He had to be really sharp for the Tommy Hearns fight in September. At the gym, Janks Morton, Sugar Ray and Angelo began preparations for the Hearns fight. This was the big one, the fight to unify the two different boxing federations' welterweight world titles. They were going to make sure there would be only one welterweight champion of the world, and he would be Sugar Ray Leonard. Angelo knew how hard Ray had been working those past three years. Nine fights in 1979, including a world welterweight title win over Wilfredo Benitez. That's some tough schedule. Yet Ray still managed a social life and kept his sense of humour, albeit sometimes a little offbeat. While he was being interviewed on television, Ray was asked by the interviewer to tell him something about the tough world of boxing that he found funny.

Ray thought for a moment then gave a quick giggle before starting his story: 'You know, in boxing, after a few rounds you start to sweat. I like sweating in a fight. I mean really sweat. It's true, I like it. Well, sometimes – not often, mind – you forget to go to the restroom before the fight. Or maybe you've left it till it's too late. You know what I mean? I'm talking about relieving yourself.' Ray chuckled and so did the interviewer. 'You know what I'm talking about, a pee-pee. So the fight starts and then it hits you: you wanna go. So you hold it in. But it gets worse. You're busting. What can you do? Right? By now you're really sweating. Your boxing shorts are soaking wet. So what do you do? You guessed it. Who knows? No one can tell. Nothing shows. That's why I never mind sweating.' Ray was grinning and the interviewer laughed so much he couldn't speak.

Ray's charismatic personality is no act, although he had aspirations in that field for a while and appeared in a few B movies. It wasn't Ray's style, though. He's an A movie man. He was a snappy dresser and he had the body and looks to carry it off. When he was a minor celebrity he looked and carried himself like a star. He was polite, friendly, and unassuming. It seemed everyone liked Angelo Dundee and Ray imitated his style in many ways. His feelings of self-belief ran deep. Ray showed people respect and he demanded it back. True, on occasions his emotions ruled his brain – the first Robert Duran fight showed that – but most times he was in control and one of the most difficult things in life for Ray Leonard to do was to wave the white flag or surrender.

As the Leonard–Hearns fight date of 16 September 1981 grew closer, an unexpected worry fell upon Dundee's shoulders. Muhammad was coming out of retirement, once again, to fight Trevor Berbick in October, a month after the scheduled Leonard fight. This would make it the second time since Ali had relinquished his title that he decided to make a comeback. His first attempt was in October 1980. He fought his old sparring partner and now the WBC world champion, Larry Holmes. Boy, was that a mistake. Angelo joined Muhammad for the final days of training. He was delighted to see Muhammad looking sharp and trim. The delight turned to sadness during the fight. After the first few rounds, Ali began to run out of gas. He had no energy. As the fight progressed, it became heartbreaking to watch the former champ take such a beating. Not to take credit away from Larry Holmes, who is one of the best heavyweights of his era, but the man he was pummelling was only a shadow of the real Ali. What had happened to him? Eventually, Dundee stopped the fight. Later, Muhammad confessed to his mentor that he had been taking thyroid pills to help him lose weight. He had sabotaged his strength. After the fight, Ali announced his retirement – again.

So it is no mystery why Dundee was concerned about the

upcoming Ali–Berbick fight. He believed Ali couldn't win, though he knew Ali would come back in great shape, without the aid of any diet pills. It was just that Muhammad was 39 years old, and no matter what you think you can do, you can't beat the ravages of age. Berbick, who idolised Ali, was a good fighter and had based his style on Ali, but he was a professional and would give his best to win. Dundee, along with millions of fight fans, wished Ali would stay in retirement. With memories of the Holmes fight still fresh in their minds, many were concerned Muhammad might suffer a serious injury.

The Ali–Berbick fight was getting little publicity. The media and the boxing enthusiasts were firmly focused on the Sugar Ray Leonard–Tommy 'Hit Man' Hearns upcoming unification championship fight. No one was more focused than Leonard, Morton and Dundee, who were busy plotting for a victory.

CHAPTER 22

'A knock out?'

Angelo didn't care what the media said – Ray was going to win, and win by a knockout. He had watched Hearns fight Pipino Cuevas and had been impressed, but Ray wasn't going to fight the way Cuevas had fought Hearns. Why would he? Cuevas lost. Ray would fight and win. A lot of people were going to get a big surprise.

Ray and Angelo had watched videotapes of Hearns in action, but due to Tommy's record of quick knockouts there was not a lot to watch. Angelo even studied photographs looking for any sign of weakness. For nearly two years, the media and matchmakers had been trying to get Angelo to let Ray fight Tommy, but he ignored it. Angelo was waiting for the right time – that is, a time that was right for Ray. Putting off that fight for so long was one of Angelo Dundee's smartest moves. He had watched Hearns stop Pedro Rojas in Detroit, two years earlier, and Tommy had looked too big and physical for Ray. There was no hurry. Wait until the time was right.

As Hearns progressed, Angelo knew that eventually Ray would have to confront him. Angelo stalled, he watched and prepared. He arranged for Ray to fight against big, tall, Marcos Geraldo in

Louisiana in May 1979. Ray tore him apart. After Ray's baptism of fire from the two Roberto Duran fights, Angelo knew he was ready for anyone and that included Thomas Hearns. The bout was made. At last, the two most popular welterweights in the world were going to meet. Perhaps the most popular fighters in the world at any weight.

Sugar Ray Leonard going against Tommy 'Hit Man' Hearns seemed to have captured the imagination of fight fans even more than the Thrilla in Manilla. A week before the fight, a television crew arrived at the gym in Miami to interview Angelo before he left to join Ray at the training camp. Angelo told the TV reporter that Ray was going to win, and win by a knockout. 'A knockout?' the reporter repeated incredulously.

'That's right,' Dundee told him. 'Ray is the harder puncher.'

The interviewer's eyes glinted sceptically. Like most of the media, he could not believe that Leonard could out-punch Hearns.

The Roberto Duran–Sugar Ray fight in Montreal had been big. The return fight in Las Vegas had been even bigger, but Leonard against Hearns was extra special. The winner would be the first undisputed welterweight champion for many years. Angelo believed Ray would win as long as he did not let emotion rule his head, as he had against Duran in Montreal. Ray understood, and set his mind on being a cool, calm and thinking fighting machine.

Unquestionably, Hearns was a tough character, 6 feet 2 inches tall – about three or four inches taller than Ray – and the possessor of a long, left lead that whipped out like a cobra. Hearns could punch, too. His fight record proved that. He would take some beating, but Ray believed he could do it if he stuck to his fight plan.

Of course, Tommy was confident he would be the winner. It was shaping up to be an exciting and unpredictable fight.

Only Caesar's Palace could have had the inspiration to convert a hotel parking lot into a fabulous, open air arena with all the myriad of facilities needed to stage a televised, world title fight. It was a monumental task. Everyone connected with the promotion was acutely aware of their responsibilities. It was a sobering thought knowing the fight would be seen on live and closed circuit television practically all over the world. As far as Ray, Janks and Angelo were concerned, they were ready. Ray was going to win.

On the night of the fight, just as the combatants and their teams entered the ring, the noise from the crowd rose to a crescendo. It was deafening. Angelo's adrenaline was flowing like it had when he had made similar walks with Muhammad Ali. He was back in Caesar's Palace. The venue had given him both success and failure. What would it bring tonight? Ray looked out at the sea of faces, soaking up the incredible atmosphere. It seemed as if his eardrums would burst from the shouting, yelling and whistling that erupted from the crowd. He couldn't analyze how he felt, but he had the same excitement he had experienced at the second Roberto Duran fight. He loved the feeling.

Angelo felt he could taste the excitement and tension. It was an atmosphere he knew and loved. It was part of the magic that comes with a big-time, controversial, world title fight. It was the Super Bowl, the World Cup Soccer Final. We know how affected we, the fans, are. Can we even start to imagine the feelings of those in the cauldron of the competition?

Ray took a deep breath, exhaled and immediately calmed down. He forgot about the crowd. He hardly heard the noise. He was completely focused on the job at hand. As the referee gave Hearns and Leonard their last minute instructions, they held a staring contest. Neither looked away. Ray felt Angelo's calming presence at his side. The two warriors touched gloves. The fight was about to begin. A wave of positive energy washed over Ray. He felt he was made for this night.

Angelo sensed Ray's confidence. It was justified. Ray had done his training with the kind of dedication Angelo had come to expect from him. Ray was ready, and Angelo, as usual, was aware that once the bell rang for the first round, Ray would be standing alone. All his encouragement, advice and tactical knowledge would only be an aid. Ray would be the guy getting hurt, soaking up the pain and punishment. Everything would depend on the skill, bravery and the will to win of the combatants. Which one would it be?

It was near the end of the fifth round. Angelo wanted it over. He didn't like the look of Ray's left eye. He could even see the swelling from the corner where he anxiously waited for the round to end. He quickly looked at Janks Morton, whose expression showed his concern. His big, heavily muscled body was tight with tension as he wiped his perspiring forehead with a slow, deliberate stroke. Janks never took his eyes off the two protagonists for a second. He and Angelo would hide their anxiety from Ray, although they were worried sick about the angry bruise under Ray's eye. Would the swelling get worse and impair Ray's vision? Trying to fight Hearns with only half vision was not a course of action any sane person would recommend.

Ray had looked good in the first few rounds. He had been cool and had done all Angelo had asked of him. Ray was making himself a most difficult target to hit, moving laterally in either direction,

187

which exposed Hearn's slowness when he moved to the left. Ray's superb reflexes enabled him to slip punches and score with counter punches, but by no means had he taken a commanding lead. In fact, Angelo admitted later, he thought Hearns was ahead on points. However, until the swelling appeared under Ray's eye, he had no doubts Ray would win, and win by a knockout.

As soon as the bell rang at the end of the round and Ray was sitting on the stool, Angelo began working on the eye. He had one minute to do what had to be done. He scrutinised the bruising, fervently hoping he had enough time. Something had happened months before in New Jersey that was to play an important part in the final result of the Hearns–Leonard title fight. While on a visit to New Jersey, Angelo was introduced to a Dr Michael Sabia, a charming and articulate man who was a big fight fan. He told Angelo of his studies into the prevention of cuts and the healing of skin tissue that had been damaged during a bout. At the end of their conversation, Dr Sabia gave Angelo a gift of a product he had designed to contain and disperse bruising. He called his product the apt name of 'Enswell'. It was made of stainless steel for temperature retention. It was about three inches long and half an inch wide. It looked a little like a modern, flat cigarette lighter. Angelo had a hunch about it and decided to take it with him on the night of the Hearns–Leonard fight. He'll never know whether it was good judgment or good luck.

Angelo sponged Ray's face, washing away the sweat, then gently dried him with a towel. The bruising was under the left eye on the cheekbone, the same cheekbone that had sustained a slight injury during training. One of his sparring partners had been a little clumsy and had inadvertently hit Ray on the cheekbone with his elbow. At the time, they did not make a big deal out of it because it wasn't serious, but it had obviously made that area sensitive. Hearns had landed a blow on the exact spot. Angelo delicately covered the swelling with a thin layer of vaseline. Then he reached into the bucket and took out the Enswell that had been cushioned between two ice packs. He placed the stainless steel on the swelling. The metal retained the cold temperature of the ice pack and was soothing and numbing to the bruised area. He began applying a little pressure, smoothing the bruise away from the potential danger area – the upper part of the lower lid which, if bruised, would close the eye.

The bell sounded for round six. No more time for repairs. Angelo had contained the bruising temporarily. 'Go to work, Ray,' he said. He didn't mention the eye. Why worry Ray. 'Let's go for it,' he said, as Ray went back onto the battlefield.

Ray moved into top gear and was catching Hearns, hurting him. Was Tommy going to tumble? Tactically, the fight had turned around. Hearns was backing away and Ray was now the aggressor. Even the atmosphere in the arena had changed. Hearns's fans were a little quieter, Leonard's a lot louder.

In between each successive round, Angelo worked on the eye. Rounds six, seven and eight passed, and although ugly and painful, the swelling had not affected Ray's vision. Enswell was doing its job, but time was not on Ray's side. Rounds nine through eleven, Ray looked tired and had noticeably slowed down. The fight was swinging back in Hearns's favour. Tommy was back in the fight. Both men were supremely conditioned athletes. It seemed there would be no let-up.

Ray slumped onto the stool at the end of round 12. He looked near exhaustion. It had been a frustrating round for him. Angelo could sense the fight slipping away. They needed a knockout to make certain. Even if Ray won the next three rounds, it was going to be a close call. Instinctively, Angelo knew Ray needed to be motivated. 'You gotta do it now, Ray.' Dundee's voice got louder and more urgent. 'You're blowing it. You hear me? You can take him out. You gotta do it now.'

The bell sounded and Ray came alive. He caught Hearns with a long right. Hearns was in trouble. Ray was all over him. There was a flurry of punches. Hearns was falling through the ropes, but the referee decided it wasn't a knock-down. Somehow, Tommy managed to survive round 13. As the bell sounded for the start of the 14th round, Ray ran over to Hearns and began throwing punches. He was in overdrive. Ray was oblivious to the strength–sapping 97 degree temperature. He had the power that comes when you sense the kill, the energy that comes with the knowledge that you are going to win. Ray swarmed all over Hearns, who was in desperate trouble. He lay helplessly on the ropes, bravely refusing to quit. Finally, the referee stepped in between the fighters, saving a courageous Hearns from further punishment. The fight was over. Sugar Ray Leonard was the undisputed welterweight champion of the world.

Sugar Ray had earned more money for one fight than any other fighter before him in the history of boxing. At that time, he was the most charismatic and popular fighter in the world. Ray was a superstar champion. Angelo embraced and congratulated the new champion before he was surrounded and overwhelmed by a bunch of photographers, reporters, television interviewers and well-wishers. Angelo was exhausted, drained. He watched the frenetic scene going on in the ring – jubilation and despair. He went over and paid his respects to the exhausted Tommy Hearns, who was heartbroken. Angelo knew how he felt. Ferdie Pacheco, the 'Fight Doctor', was interviewing Sugar Ray for television. Angelo stood by Ray's side and listened as Ray, holding a towel over the badly bruised eye, gave his accurate comments on the fight. Angelo was turning to go when a restraining hand on his arm stopped him. A voice whispered in his, 'Ferdie wants an interview.'

Ferdie Pacheco, a friend who had worked with Angelo through the Muhammad Ali years, turned towards him and began the interview. He ended by saying that Angelo had been right in saying before the fight that Leonard was the better puncher. Angelo smiled and began to leave as Ferdie added, 'Congratulations, Angelo, on a brilliant victory in a brilliant career.'

CHAPTER 23

There's always a last round

Muhammad had come out of retirement to fight Larry Holmes. He lost then retired. He then changed his mind, came out of retirement once more, and agreed to fight in the Bahamas against the young, strong Trevor Berbick. This was going to be just a few months after the Sugar Ray–Tommy Hearns fight. Another emotional night lay ahead for Angelo. The Ali–Berbick fight took place on 11 December. Ali lost – he would most certainly have won in his prime. Naturally, Angelo was in Ali's corner on that sad night when, after the loss, he finally retired for good. Angelo did not consider it a sad night. He pointed out, 'Muhammad wanted one more chance at the glory. He was 39 years of age with the enthusiasm of a teenager. Why not let the guy roll the dice once more? I'm glad he finally did retire. I wish he had remained retired after he won back his title, but no. He was the best thing that ever happened to boxing! They weren't kidding when they called him "The Greatest". If he wanted one more fight, he was entitled.'

They had gone through a roller coaster ride together and a special bond had developed between them. Whenever you see Dundee and

Ali together, their genuine affection for one another is palpable. In some ways, they were similar. Their sense of humour and their cavalier approach to financial acquisition – in other words, accumulating money, or ostentatiously displaying or hoarding wealth, was not part of their being. Muhammad gave away millions of dollars to various charities. On one occasion, he visited a Jewish old folk's home in Miami. None of the aged residents had a television set so Muhammad stepped in and bought one for each and every one of them. No press. No photo opportunity. Houston McTear, an amateur track star, had wonderful parents. They had sacrificed everything to support their son's amateur athletic career and ended up living in poverty. Muhammad stepped in and bought them a house. Again, no fuss, no media.

In his early days, Angelo had a predilection for gambling and was also generous to his young fighters. Betty Mitchell, his long-serving office manager, revealed that if she had all the money Angelo had lost gambling, plus the considerable amount he had loaned, advanced, given away – call it what you will – to his young fighters, she could retire for life.

There is no doubt, many people thought Muhammad's retirement came too late. There were rumours he was sick. And he was. After his retirement, he was diagnosed as suffering with hypoglycemia – an inadequate supply of glucose in the blood. Both Dundee and Muhammad accepted that the hypoglycemia was the cause of his listlessness, fatigue and frequent bouts of unusual thirst.

By 1982, many media stories debating Muhammad's state of health, partially fuelled by Dr Ferdi Pacheco's opinion given back in 1977, as he left the team, that Ali had taken on one too many fights and too many blows to the head, causing the once-great fighter brain damage. In July 1982, Muhammad visited the Allen Street Gym, in North Miami, used by Angelo for training his fighters. The author was fortunate enough to have been there and it was both a pleasure and an education. For three rounds, Muhammad and Reiner Hartman, a young German heavyweight Dundee was training, sparred together without wearing boxing gloves or actually hitting each other. It was like a choreographed ballet, but of course it wasn't. At its finish, the folks in the gym erupted in applause. At the end of three rounds of three minutes each, Ali was sweating – but so was the young German. After the sparring, Muhammad sat on an old wooden chair and gave an interview to a local television reporter. He had been tipped off about Muhammad's impromptu visit by Betty Mitchell, acting on Muhammad's own instructions. Some secret visit!

It would seem Ali missed the spotlight, or he wanted to get some publicity for Angelo, the gym and Angelo's new, young fighters. Perhaps both – that would be a safe bet. When the TV interviewer had gone, Muhammad remained sitting where he was, still sweating from the sparring session. Angelo took the wet towel draped around his neck and shoulders, and replaced it with a clean one. There were around 20 people in the gym. A few locals who had seen the TV vehicle outside the gym were curious and the teenagers using the basketball area at the back of the building had sauntered into the gym to see what was going on.

Muhammad began addressing the small crowd. Strictly impromptu. It was vintage Ali. Inspiring, funny, witty and knowledgeable. He ended his monologue by telling everyone that he would be coming to the gym at lunchtime for the next two weeks, and they should bring the children. They did, and he was there too, always finding the time to talk to the kids. Everyone had read the reports about Ali having brain damage but after listening to him hypnotizing the audience in the gym, it seemed there was very little wrong with his mind.

Muhammad did an interview on TV in the summer of 1984, and admitted in humility and humour that in the past few weeks he had gotten more press than Michael Jackson: Yes he did have a medical problem that was being controlled with medication, referring to hypoglycemia, and he did not have any brain damage.

This now brings us to the unavoidable and regrettable fact that Muhammad Ali does have Parkinson's disease. The symptoms of slurred speech, shaking, and impaired motor skills in general are visible, but the jump to accuse boxing is unfair and unwarranted. Being punched on the head lots of times may indeed create brain damage, but it is highly unlikely to sustain the opinion that it causes Parkinson's. Most cases of Parkinson's are due to a combination of a genetic disposition and a vulnerability to environmental toxin exposure. Cases vary geographically.

Research and reputable studies have shown that individuals exposed to pesticides had a 70 per cent higher risk of developing Parkinson's than those not exposed. The first case was described by British physician James Parkinson in 1808. Note the date – the beginning of the Industrial Revolution! There have been numerous cases caused by rural well water. Researches theorise that water consumption is a proxy for pesticide exposure. Also, there have been increases in Parkinson's in persons exposed to agricultural chemicals. Makes you think, eh?

* * *

Retirement probably never entered Sugar Ray's mind after the Hearns win. Why should it? He was not yet 26. Yet, within six months of his victory, it became a distinct possibility. In February 1982, Ray defended his undisputed title against Bruce Finch. The night before, Angelo's brother, Jimmy, lost a long battle with cancer. Angelo had got the news of his bother's death while he was with Sugar Ray in Reno for the Bruce Finch fight that was scheduled for the following night, 15 February 1982. Dundee worked Ray's corner as usual that night. He knew that was what Jimmy would have wanted. In his mind, Angelo could hear his brother telling him, 'You gotta work the corner, Angie. That's what you do, right?'

Ray KO'd Finch in three rounds. Two days later, Angelo flew back to New Jersey for Jimmy's funeral. It lifted Angelo's spirits to see Sugar Ray Leonard and his wife, Juanita, among the mourners. In the Finch fight, Ray had taken a hit to the eye. It looked harmless and didn't affect the fight. Janks Morton and Dundee thought no more about it. Leonard carried on preparing for his next defence in May, against Roger Stafford. The public was shocked when days before the fight, an eye exam showed Ray had suffered a detached retina in his left eye. It was a serious threat to Ray's eyesight. The fight was cancelled and Ray entered the John Hopkins University Hospital in Baltimore, Maryland, for surgery.

When Angelo got the news, he flew into Baltimore and was at Ray's bedside along with Janks and Leonard's family members. Dundee remembered Ray and his wife, Juanita, had taken the time to attend Jimmy's funeral. Dundee prayed silently for the operation to be successful.

Whether or not Sugar Ray would ever fight again depended on

the decision made by the specialist, who would need to wait five months or so before deciding if the surgery had been successful. It meant Dundee would spend more time with his family and his other fighters while he waited. His revised contract, the one signed unwisely in Ray's dressing room at the time of the Dave 'Boy' Green fight, had run its two-year duration. He was now completely independent, but it wasn't business ties that had brought him to Ray's bedside.

Six months after the surgery, in October, Leonard announced he was holding a press conference, and the general public who wished to attend would pay a nominal entrance fee that would be donated to charity. It was a great idea to have a charity benefit from a promotional event. The event had been well prepared, and it was obvious that a great deal of time and effort had gone into it. Dundee, like most people there, was both shocked and relieved when Sugar Ray eloquently announced his retirement from the ring. It was done with a Hollywood panache. There was even a commemorative brochure, 'An Evening with Sugar Ray Leonard'. The title was perhaps a clue to Ray's eventual showbiz future. Was Dundee annoyed he hadn't been informed earlier of Leonard's decision? Possibly. If so, what was written in the brochure would have taken away any feelings of annoyance. Sugar Ray had commented, 'Angelo respected me as a man. That was one big reason why we got along so well. His input has been invaluable to my career.'

Angelo was pleased with Ray's tribute, and he was also pleasantly surprised by the comments made by Mike Trainer. 'Throughout Ray's professional career, Dundee's impeccable knowledge of the fight game, sage advice and ringside savvy have helped build a champion.' How could Angelo not be flattered and gratified?

Champions miss the glamour, the attention, the excitement and thrill of competing. Being in the limelight can act as a drug. It's not just the fight game that's affected. Youth, celebrities and addiction seem to go together in today's society. Ray lasted the best part of two years away from the limelight. In April 1984, Trainer informed Dundee that Sugar Ray's eye was fine, and he was making a comeback, or as Ray put it, 'resuming his career in boxing.'

Sugar Ray joined Angelo in Miami for his final training sessions. He looked sharp and his appetite for work in the gym was still there, as was his charisma. The other fighters treated him like a visiting prince. He would kid around, have them laughing and put on little shows for spectators when they came in – which was often. It was like the old days when Muhammad and Willie Pastrano would light up the gym with their fun and laughter. Dundee watched Ray train and hoped the long lay-off wouldn't affect his performance in the ring. Training is one thing, but a real live fight when the opponent wants to knock you out is something else. His opponent, Kevin Howard, was game and strong.

Shortly before the contest, Leonard had a minor procedure performed on his eye. He shrugged it off, but the fight was postponed until May. Dundee, working on a fight-to-fight arrangement, wasn't judgmental. Although concerned, he knew other fighters who had fought after having corrective surgery on a partially detached retina without consequences. All he could do was think and act positively and help get Ray ready for the bout.

The fight didn't prove much, except that Ray could take a good punch. He got decked in the first round, but had the will to get off the canvas and stop the outclassed Howard in the third round. His eye suffered no injury. His ring rust showed, yet in flashes, there were glimpses of the old, brilliant Sugar Ray. Nevertheless, immediately after the fight Ray announced his retirement once again.

Leonard would make a few more 'career resumptions' before finally calling it a day. He would have another seven fights before hanging up his boxing gloves. Four of them were just paydays and allowed Sugar Ray a little more time in the spotlight. Nothing wrong with that, but Sugar Ray deserves better than to be remembered for those four fights.

The first one took place roughly three years after the Kevin Howard fight. Sugar Ray decided to have just one more bout. It was to be as big as any before it. Leonard was going to battle the WBC middleweight champion of the world. A fighter, who in the last few years, had acquired a near-legendary reputation. The name Marvin Hagler was known across the globe as a respected and worthy champion. He always came to fight and was always in top shape. He was on the list of great fighters, but not one gifted with that elusive mantle of greatness. That, maybe, was the difference between these superb athletes.

The fight took place in April 1987, a date Marvin Hagler would not forget. He felt he was robbed. It is a remarkable that Sugar Ray got the decision, though it was very close, and many disputed the decision. Traditionally, the opponent has to beat the champion without any doubts. In a questionable decision the advantage would usually go to the champion. But not this time. Notwithstanding the disagreement over the decision, Leonard, after a three-year lay–off, came up in weight to beat the best middleweight in the world at the time. Ray carved his name with emphasis in the annals of boxing history. Why did Ray believe he could beat such an opponent – if he had to fight again, why not pick an easy one? The answer was his opponents had to be on the A list, and Marvin Hagler was certainly that. After that outstanding success, once again, Ray announced his retirement.

What a perfect time to quit, but not in Sugar Ray's opinion. At the end of 1988 he decided to make another comeback. He had found another challenge he couldn't resist. It wasn't Angelo's style to discourage. If Leonard wanted him in his corner, he'd be there. This next bout was against Donny Lalonde. That night at Caesar's Palace, Las Vegas, Ray won two world titles in one night. The bout was for the newly formed WBC super middleweight title. After a shaky start, he hit the canvas only to get up and go on to knockout Lalonde in the ninth round. Ray became the new WBC super middleweight champion. Lalonde was also the WBC light heavyweight champion and that title was on the line too. But, and it was a big 'but', Mike Trainer had included in the contract that Lalonde could not fight at the light heavyweight limit of 175 pounds, so Lalonde fought at weight parity with Leonard at around 167 pounds. It was another remarkable victory for Sugar Ray. From welterweight champion to light heavyweight champion via taking the title as super welterweight, middleweight and super middleweight. Surely, this was the right time to call it a day?

Ray went on to chalk up wins in rematches with Tommy Hearns and Roberto Duran, as well as beating Terry Norris at the legendary Madison Square Garden – Ray's only fight there. Is it superfluous to mention he made another retirement announcement?

Six years passed before the fight bug struck again. It was in 1997, when retirement lost its allure. This time the venue was the Convention Center, Atlantic City, and the opponent, former world lightweight champion, Hector 'Macho' Comacho. Leonard was 40 years of age, Hector younger by six years. Apart from a morbid curiosity, most fight fans showed little interest in the bout. In the not so distant past, we had admired the outrageous Comacho, and we had idolised the great Sugar Ray Leonard. We wanted to enshrine him, not witness the pathetic remains of this once phenomenal fighter be humiliated. And this fight against Comacho was just that, a humiliation. Not known for his punching power, Hector Comacho KO'd Sugar Ray Leonard, one of the great fighters in boxing history, in five rounds. Sugar Ray finally retired. Not with a fanfare of trumpets or a triumphant parade. The former champion melted into the shadows and that last fight became a sad statistic in a record of greatness.

Muhammad Ali retired. Ray Leonard retired. Both saw action and suffered injuries. The saying goes, 'Old soldiers never die. They only fade away.' Well, these two warriors didn't fade too easily and neither did Angelo Dundee. Our two retired warriors and their trusted Sergeant went their separate ways. They had been a credit to their sport, and now, they were to continue their success in various ways, not together, but individually. Exactly what they did with their lives up to this time is for another book, but before I bring the curtain down on this one, there are some questions to answer and a few comments to be made.

Many people wonder why Muhammad and Sugar Ray carried on fighting so long. Surely they knew they were well past their 'sell by' date? Maybe they didn't know, or didn't want to believe it. The same personality traits that made them super stars – self confidence, ego, courage, pride – were perhaps responsible for the sad ending of their careers. Their reluctance to walk away from the limelight must have been fuelled by ego. That they believed they could defy age and vanquish their opponent, no matter how formidable, was caused by an excess of self confidence. Their refusal to let pain or physical exhaustion undermine their will, and to fight on when all seemed lost, displayed great courage. The physical pain they took was never as bad as the hurt their pride suffered in defeat.

Ray and Ali were two remarkable men who were fortunate enough to find the right man, perhaps the only man, who could add to and enhance their talent. It couldn't have been easy for Dundee to be constantly surrounded by personalities with such large egos, strong wills, sense of self importance, determination and a deficit of compromise, such as Mike Trainer, Herbert Muhammad and the many 'big shots' Dundee would have met and dealt with at all levels of the boxing world. Angelo's life had prepared him for this role. He had been a major force in the development of the two most charismatic boxers of their era. He was the only manager to have two successive heavyweight champions – Ali and Jimmy Ellis – and he was possibly the most honoured one in boxing, receiving over two dozen awards, and being inducted into the Boxing Hall of Fame in Syracuse, New York. What would he do without Ali and Leonard in his life? An easy question. Though in his eighties, Angelo has carried on working with boxers. He is also a consultant for Trevor Caesar in Miami and spends time at Trevor's three gyms evaluating young prospects.

The words 'professional boxing' and 'Angelo Dundee' are synonymous. He never counted the days he worked in the gym, he made sure each day counted. This book has been about three men and their relationships and aspirations. Theirs is a story that has lived in the newspaper headlines, TV programs, articles, books and even movies. Yet, after all the coverage, we don't know why Dundee was the X factor in Ali's and Leonard's phenomenal success. In fact, we still don't know what makes that special champion, or do we?

'Champions are not made in gyms. Champions are made from something they have deep inside them – a desire, a dream, a vision. They have last–minute stamina. They have to be a little faster, they have to have the will. But the will must be stronger than the skill.' Do you know who said that? It was Muhammad Ali. He is undeniably right but, after reading this book, it would be understandable if you added, 'It would be very useful to have an Angelo Dundee in your corner too.'